# ON WRITING YOUR FIRST NOVEL

The Journey of a Wannabe Novelist

---

STEPHEN HAUNTS

Copyright © 2023 Stephen Haunts
Published by Adventures in Writing. A brand of Stephen Haunts Ltd

https://www.adventuresinwriting.com/

All rights reserved. No part of this book may be reproduced or used in any manner without the prior written permission of the copyright owner, except for the use of brief quotations in a book review.

Developmental / copy editing, and proofreading by Scribendi

Manuscript version 1.0

To request permissions, contact the publisher at www.adventuresinwriting.com/contact

Paperback: 978-1-9169067-6-1
Ebook: 978-1-9169067-7-8

*This book is dedicated to my wife Amanda, and my children Amy and Daniel.*

## About the Author

Stephen Haunts is a writer who lives in Derbyshire in the United Kingdom with his wife and two children. Stephen and his family are fans of theme-parks and rollercoasters. He's happiest when hanging upside down, and hurtling along a rollercoaster track at 100kph, or sitting at his desk writing novels.

# Contents

1. Introduction — 1
2. What Took Me So Long? — 4
3. What Changed? — 11
4. Why Creative Writing? — 16
5. What I am trying to Write — 26
6. My Writing Tools — 36
7. Jumping on the Learning Train — 43
8. Story Planning — 48
9. Finding the Time to Write — 62
10. Writers Block — 67
11. Getting Feedback While You Write — 71
12. Self-Doubt After the Honeymoon Period — 79
13. My Writing Process — 90
14. Mental and Physical Health when Writing — 94
15. Positive Mental Attitude — 103
16. The Danger of Comparison — 116
17. Getting to the First Draft Finish Line — 120
18. Climbing the Self-Editing Mountain — 124
19. Working With a Professional Editor — 143
20. Book Formatting — 156
21. Blurb Writing and Marketing Copy — 166
22. Cover Design — 177
23. Post Implementation Review — 189

Thank You — 200
Please Leave a Review — 201
Appendices — 202
Appendix 1 - Airlock Escape Short Story — 203
Appendix 2 - Dealing with Criticism — 215
Appendix 3 - How to Give Constructive Criticism — 223
Diary of a Martian Extract — 233
Prologue — 235

Chapter 1: Football Practice 240
Chapter 2: Chip Reset 247
Chapter 3: Unity Day 253
Chapter 4: The Protest 258

ONE

## Introduction

During the COVID-19 pandemic of 2020–2021, I thought it would be a good idea to write a novel—a middle-grade, science fiction children's novel called *Diary of a Martian*. I started writing this book (*On Writing Your First Novel*) at the same time because trying to write just one book at a time clearly wouldn't be difficult enough.

When I started writing *On Writing Your First Novel*, I was about 20,000 words into my novel. By the time I finish this book, I will have finished writing *Diary of a Martian*, which will be around seventy to 80,000 words.

*On Writing Your First Novel* is about the journey of taking an idea and developing it into a finished novel. Ever since I was in my early twenties (I am forty-six at the time of writing), I liked the idea of writing a novel. I had plenty of ideas, but I kept putting it off. There were many reasons, which I will go into in Chapter One, but looking back, delaying writing is one of the few regrets I have. It's easy to say in retrospect, but some of my reasons for delaying, which felt valid at the time, seem silly now.

I hope I can spare you the same regret and give you back many years of writing.

## What Not to Expect from this Book

There are hundreds, if not thousands, of books on the craft of writing novels. I know, because I have read many of them. A lot of these books follow a similar pattern. A chapter on 'show, don't tell'. A chapter on characters. A chapter on scenes, world-building, conflict and so on. These are all very important subjects, and I recommend that you read some of these books. But you won't find that pattern in this book.

## What to Expect from this Book

In this book, I am going to talk about the process I went through to plan and write my novel. I will discuss the challenges I faced and how I overcame them. I am not perfect, and *Diary of a Martian* is my first novel. I will make mistakes, but I wanted to document what I learned. A lot of what I write in this book is my opinion. This isn't a step-by-step how-to guide. You may agree with what I say or you may not. If you don't, that's fine. Just treat what I say as an alternative viewpoint. Alternative viewpoints are still useful to read about, even if you disagree. In either case, I thank you for reading.

## Previous Experience

I should declare that I have written and published several nonfiction books, so I am not new to writing and publishing, although novel writing is new to me. I have published some of my books through large publishers, and others I have published myself.

Writing a nonfiction book is different from writing a novel. The types of nonfiction books I write are instructional, where I am teaching the reader how to accomplish something. When working with a traditional publisher for nonfiction, you write a detailed outline of the book and provide a writing sample, after which, the book gets commissioned, if you are lucky. Once you have signed the contract, you write the book to an agreed schedule.

Writing a novel is different. No publisher is likely to sign up a book on an idea alone—not unless you are a celebrity with a vast audience. When you write a novel, you complete the book, perform several revisions, hire an editor and, once you are finished, try to find an agent who will then try to sell the book to a publisher. You can, of course, publish the book yourself, which I talk about near the end of this book.

These steps might make it sound easy, but writing a novel is hard: very hard! Much harder than the nonfiction books I have written. Your plot must be fun and engaging. Your characters need to be likeable and convincing. The setting and world-building need to be rich and imaginative. As the writer, you need to hold so many details in your head—or written down—to ensure the entire story makes sense. I can honestly say that writing my first novel has been the most challenging project I have worked on in a twenty-eight-year career, but it has also been one of the most rewarding.

TWO

## What Took Me So Long?

The desire to write a novel has lingered with me since my early twenties. I had plenty of ideas, but I procrastinated. When I was at school, written English was never my forte. In fact, I hated English lessons. We read books I didn't like and wrote essays on subjects I found boring. I was also quite stubborn and didn't give much attention to subjects I wasn't interested in. It didn't help that my English teacher and I didn't see eye to eye. Looking back, I think there's a good chance that I was the problem and not the teacher.

Though I enjoyed reading novels as a teenager, I didn't read as much as I should have. Instead, I was out with my friends or playing video games. After I finished university, started my career and settled down in my early twenties, I started reading more books again: science fiction, fantasy, spy thrillers, horror. I enjoy most genre fiction novels, though I'm not so keen on romantic fiction or literary fiction; they are just not my thing.

As I read more books, ideas for my own stories emerged. I've always had an active imagination and loved the thought of writing my own stories. Some people want to be rock stars. To me, being a novelist seemed more fun. Still, I had many excuses for not starting, many of which I now regret. Hindsight can be great for uncovering regrets.

## Intimidated by Other Books

One problem when wanting to start a creative endeavour is that it is easy to compare your ideas to those of others. Whenever I picked up another author's novel to read, I was always struck by how flawless it seemed. The plots were well thought out. The grammar seemed perfect. The quality was high. It was intimidating! How could I ever do the same?

What I didn't understand at the time was the process an author goes through to write a novel. I had attempted to write short stories before, and although I was pleased with them, the writing didn't seem as good as what I read in other novels. Maybe I just didn't have the skills to produce something of the same quality? My short stories were shelved as first drafts.

If I had done my research, I'd have learned that an author will write a first draft and that draft will not be very good. They will then do a full revision. Then they'll do another and another. This revision process can go on and on until the author has a draft they are happy with. This revised version is the real first draft. Even at that point, the book is not finished. If the author has signed with an agent or sold the book to a publisher, the manuscript will then undergo a further series of revisions with a professional editor.

Once the publisher's editor has finished, there is a final stage of revisions, which consists of the copy edit and proofread. Your book may go through ten to fifteen revisions before it is published and in the hands of your readers. No wonder published novels are of high quality! The text has been revised, tweaked and moulded over a long time to reach that level. So, of course, my first draft stories didn't seem as good. I hadn't gone through the entire process.

## Worried My Ideas Were Bad

I thought my book ideas were good, but I think everyone thinks that. What worried me was what other people might think of my ideas. People can be cruel. You just need to look at reviews on Amazon to see that. Even for popular books, the one- and two-star reviews show that people can be very nasty, especially when hidden behind online anonymity.

Being criticised is scary. Nobody likes it. But now that I am older and a little wiser, I am not so worried about it. If I get a negative review for something, and there are lots of other positive reviews, then I just assume that the book wasn't to someone's taste. I now believe that if you do the best work you can, go through the revision steps, use a professional editor, and take their advice, the product you put into the marketplace will be good. If someone doesn't like it, well, that's on them.

As I mentioned before, I have released some nonfiction books and have practical experience with all the steps I've mentioned. I went through all the steps related to revision with my nonfiction books and released the best books I could. I know they are good, and the reviews are mostly very good. So, while the occasional negative review still hurts, I have learnt to brush them off. If the reviews are not offensive, I try to learn from them.

## Scared by the Amount of Work

When I was younger, I was a little intimidated by the amount of work required to write a book—and that was just to get to the first draft stage. I liked the idea of having written a book, but it seemed like so much work. As someone once said to me, 'you want to reach the destination, but you don't want to undertake the journey'.

I will bet that this is a common problem for anyone looking to tackle an enormous project like a novel. As a young man, I was not experienced in planning a large project. With over twenty-eight years of industry experience working on huge software development projects, I now tackle a book project like any of my former corporate software projects: with lots of planning and breaking the project down into smaller pieces. It's like the joke, 'How do you eat an elephant? One bite at a time'. That is so true.

Take this book, for example. I am attempting to write this while writing my first novel. I have a big head start on the novel, but it probably seems crazy to write a second book at the same time. Well, it's not that bad. I spent a month planning what I wanted in this book. I came up with a chapter plan that mapped out what I wanted to say. Then I went through each chapter and outlined each subheading. Once I had done that, as I started writing each chapter, I would make notes under each subheading to make sure I was clear about my message.

Thanks to this planning, I knew what I wanted to write ahead of writing the actual book. This is a linear nonfiction book. Outlining books like this is not that hard. I know that because I have the outline open in front of me. Outlining a novel is much harder, and I will cover that later in the book. Take this chapter, for example. You will notice I split it into subheadings. Each of those headings started out in rough note form and then, over the space of a few days, was filled in.

I did not write this book in one go. I did a little each day: not much, maybe 200–500 words on average, sometimes over a thousand, if I was in the zone—just chipping away at the text and following the outline. I put a higher priority on the actual novel, but, on some days, if I was stuck and wasn't sure how to tackle part of the story, I would stop and jump across to this book for a while. The very act of doing something else would help me get unstuck with the story, as I left my brain alone to process the problem in the background. Likewise, if I was stuck on this book, which happened from time to time, I had some short story ideas to chip away at.

By focusing on just a little at a time, before you know it, you will have completed that gigantic project. I experienced this first-hand with one of my nonfiction books, a business and entrepreneurial book called *The Path to Freedom – Starting a Business for the Reluctant Entrepreneur*. The final manuscript was 150,000 words. That's an enormous book. But I applied the same principle to that book as to this book: detailed outlining and working on a small piece at a time. The book took eighteen months to write, but I wasn't daunted by the size of the project because I had broken it down into much smaller pieces. I believe that if any project scares you, you haven't broken it down far enough.

## Busy Learning Software Development

Like most career-minded professionals in their twenties, I was trying to build up my job skills, which, for me, were in software development. I started my career in the video games industry and, after eight years, moved into financial services as a software developer and then through the ranks as a leader. My career wasn't writing novels—that was just a dream, though a nice one to have.

Even though I have regrets about not starting a novel earlier in life, I don't have regrets about focusing on my career. You need the career to help provide for your family, put a roof over your head and make sure everyone has what they need. Building a stable career is very hard, so while I include career building in my reasons for not starting a novel, this one is justified.

## Starting a Family Took Up My Time

I don't regret building up a decent career, and I also don't regret having children. I have two: Amy, and Daniel. If you are reading this and you have young children, then you'll agree that they are fun, yet very tiring. Bringing up children is exhausting. My wife and I found two children hard work. Anyone who can raise three or more deserves a medal.

When you find a little spare time as a parent and want to write or take part in some other creative exploit, you may be tired and uninspired; I know I was. This constant level of fatigue also contributed to not wanting to start a novel. All the other reasons I stated in this chapter were the primary reasons, but being tired with children was the perfect excuse, and one with which I don't think anyone would argue.

Now that my children are a little older, they are not as demanding. We do lots of activities as a family, but they also want to play with their friends, have sleepovers, play video games and so forth, so my wife and I find we have more time for activities together and our own projects. As a little motivation for parents of younger children, it gets easier, I promise.

## Key Takeaways

This chapter, which was quite personal to me, explained why I delayed creative writing for so long. Most people act more quickly. I know many people now who are much younger than I and are prolific writers. The key takeaway here is that if you find yourself making excuses for not writing for any reason—not just those I described—then your best bet is to start writing.

I began with short stories, as they are self-contained mini projects.

Don't worry about quality while drafting. Just write, and always try to finish what you start. The result doesn't have to be great. First drafts rarely are. But once you have that first draft, you have something to work with, to edit, experiment with, knock into shape. As the saying goes, you can't edit an empty page. It may be many months before you tackle the story again, but eventually you will reach a result you are happy with.

Now you know why I put off starting my novel for so long. Perhaps you have read this chapter thinking that these are just excuses for inaction. You would be correct; they are. That's why many are regrets.

So, what changed? What made me stop procrastinating and start working on this novel?

THREE

## What Changed?

The year 2020 started off like any other. I was running my business and creating online training courses. Life was good. Then, in March, the COVID-19 pandemic hit, and the whole of the United Kingdom—like many other countries—went into lockdown. Like many people, I had to get used to working from home while trying to home-school two children.

As the pandemic raged on, I wanted to turn my hand to something different from my work as a distraction from everything going on around me. Home-schooling was stressful, especially when fit in around work. I needed something fresh and exciting to focus on and help me deal with the new daily routine.

I started my career working in the video game industry in the late 1990s and stayed in this field for many years. Early in the pandemic, I thought it would be fun to work on a small game engine. I did this for a few months, and it *was* fun. But the problem is that, to create anything meaningful in video gaming, you need the help of many other people, such as visual artists and designers. In the midst of a pandemic, doing anything that involved working with anyone else just didn't seem like a good idea. People couldn't meet up in person, and even if someone agreed to work on a small lockdown project, they would most likely be distracted by the pandemic; I wouldn't blame them.

I have always enjoyed creating and building things. Computer code, music, video editing, cooking. I like it all. Creativity makes me happy. So, I wondered. How could I continue to fuel this creativity with the constraints of the pandemic? What could I do that doesn't require anyone else to be involved, that is challenging enough to be satisfying and could have a result I can share with the world? It didn't take me long to think about creative writing. I had already written and published nonfiction books for my work, both through traditional publishers and independently. And, of course, that early desire to write a novel hadn't entirely disappeared.

I hadn't entertained the idea of creative writing for at least seven years. While I had the regrets I discussed in the previous chapter, I wasn't sitting around thinking about my desire to write a novel. I was busy with other aspects of my life and career. However, the pandemic opened an interesting opportunity for me. Creative writing was something I could study and practise that required no input from anyone else, which was a benefit when the world was locked down. I got straight to work, ordering books on writing and watching courses online.

This new desire to learn about writing transformed into another higher-level goal: to leave lockdown better than when I went in. I was going to study and practise a new skill to open new and fun opportunities later. I already had some sense of how difficult this writing process would be, compared with writing and publishing nonfiction books. I expected a novel to be much harder as there are so many more aspects to monitor, such as plot, subplots, characters and their motivations and world-building. I decided that writing short stories might be a good place to start. Short stories meant I could practise writing well-crafted and formatted prose but on a smaller scale than a novel and with a project that's easier to complete. With the pressures of lockdown in place, narrowing the scope felt like a good idea.

One of the first decisions I needed to make was: What was I going to write, and for whom? I knew what I didn't want to write: romantic stories. I also didn't want to write literary fiction; some of those books make my head hurt. I wanted to write stories that were easy to read. Genre fiction is sometimes accused of not being literary enough, but I'm fine with that because, when I read a book, I am reading for fun, and commercial genre fiction books are fun. I always enjoyed science fiction, fantasy, horror and thrillers, so doing something in one of those genres made sense.

Partway through the lockdown, I came across an advert on Instagram for an online video training site called Masterclass, which is a service that produces training courses by celebrities and experts in a field. What attracted me to the site was their courses by authors. Their platform included authors like Neil Gaiman, Margaret Atwood, James Patterson, David Baldacci, Dan Brown and R. L. Stine. I watched all the classes with famous authors over the space of a few weeks in the evenings. Each course was insightful, but the one that grabbed my attention the most was by R. L. Stine, the creator of the Goosebumps and Fear Street series for children and young adults.

In one section of the course, Stine talked about writing for middle-grade audiences, which is a reading age from nine to twelve years old. He said something that caught my attention.

Stine stated that, in this reading range, many readers are developing advanced vocabularies and a higher reading ability. Readers in this age group are also very good at suspending disbelief and enjoying a story, no matter how weird and wacky it is. In Stine's opinion, this is the last age group in which you can have a lot of fun with the stories.

I figured that I should look at targeting middle-grade science fiction and fantasy. I started reading around the subject and came up with ideas for a few stories. My first story was about identical twin sisters who use their identical appearances to hatch a plan to cheat on a test at school. I wrote another story about a boy who travels back in time with his dad's time machine and teaches prehistoric people how to light fires and about what had happened to society when the boy travels forward in time again. In 2020, I wrote nine short stories and was very pleased with them.

Focusing on short stories helped me learn how to format prose. As each story was short—fewer than 4,000 words—I had a sense of completion with each project, which was very satisfying.

## Key Takeaways

Creative writing is a fantastic way to work on a project that doesn't require the help or input of anyone else, apart from at the editing and proofing stages at the end of the project. I know this goes counter to most productivity books that talk about the importance of collaboration and teamwork, but sometimes it's just nice to work on something by yourself. It's yours. You own it. During a lockdown and a pandemic, this felt more important than ever.

Stretching yourself to learn new skills is very rewarding. The journey of learning a new craft or hobby, like creative writing, can be just as fun as the actual writing itself.

When beginning any creative project that you are inexperienced with, starting small is a benefit. In my case, I spent a while with short stories before even attempting to write a novel. The practice of writing short stories was fulfilling. Even while writing a novel, I still write short stories.

FOUR

# Why Creative Writing?

When the COVID-19 lockdowns started, like many people, I felt quite depressed and suffered from anxiety, as I couldn't see an end to the pandemic; this would not be over in a few weeks. As the lockdown dragged on, I started having a bit of an existential crisis, questioning everything I had done in my life. These were not the healthiest thoughts, but this is what a pandemic will do to you. As someone who generally has a very positive outlook, I wrote down my thoughts, intending to turn them into a positive.

What the pandemic taught me was just how fragile life can be. Entering 2020, most of us were expecting the year to be ordinary, but that normality was taken away from us and a huge number of people lost their lives. Among the dark thoughts I had was, 'If I were to die today, how would I be remembered?'

I have had a successful career. I have worked on many interesting projects, but I also realised that pretty much everything I have worked on doesn't exist anymore. For example, I started my career in the video game industry from 1997 to 2005. I was a software developer, and I worked on some fun games. But none of those games are for sale anymore, and the platform/consoles we developed them on are no longer current. Copies of the games still exist, but you can't buy them new anymore. You can play some through emulators, but that is a lot of effort. While I have no regrets about those projects, they are now just a blip in history.

Once I left the game industry, I went into financial services as a software developer. For six years, I worked at one of the United Kingdom's first digital-only banks and helped launch many products. It was very fulfilling. But the company was acquired and eventually closed, meaning everything I worked on no longer exists. None of that code is running anymore.

In my current day job, I run a small (single person) business creating corporate online training courses. This is work that I am very proud of, but again, if I stop maintaining those courses, over time, they will disappear from existence.

I am not unique in having these thoughts. It's the same story in most people's careers. Much of what we work on, over time, will cease to exist. In my anxiety-induced state during the pandemic, that was bothering me. Yet these thoughts helped spur me into learning the craft of creative writing and taking it seriously. These thoughts added fuel to my creative fire. They gave me a new creative purpose.

What I like about writing and its final output, books, is that the medium can live on forever, either as physical paper books or eBooks. Unlike video games, where the platforms they run on become obsolete and require significant care and attention to remain running with emulators, a book is just text. I still own books I had as a child. They may be a little dog-eared, but they still work. I can pick them up and read them just as I did back then. Even with eBooks, they are just text files, so as time marches on, they will still be available to read. On my Kindle, I can read a classic Charles Dickens or Lewis Carroll novel or, on the same device, open the latest Stephen King or James Patterson thriller.

I like the idea that I can write stories that my own children can read—and they have enjoyed my short stories. Beyond that, however, I love the idea that my children could share the same stories with their own children in the future. The technology of physical books and eBooks being ubiquitous, stories can live on for a very long time. To me, this makes it feel like the act of writing short stories, or a novel, has purpose. Everything else I have worked on in my life, while providing a good living for my family and me, was transient; they only existed for a limited period.

My worry about the lifespan of creative endeavours likely has something to do with being in my forties. Many people who enter their mid-life years have similar thoughts about their meaning and relevance to the world. I never used to worry about issues like this, but it has taken being older and in a very restrictive pandemic to make me re-evaluate what's important.

With this new creative fire lit in my soul, I set about learning my craft and writing short stories. I consumed many books about writing, watched hundreds of hours of content on YouTube and devoured online training courses. I immersed myself in the technical and creative craft of writing.

## Personal Writing Commandments

With all this preparation under my belt, I set about defining my personal commandments for my writing. Establishing a series of commandments helps me solidify why I am doing this. These commandments will be important later when I have finished writing the book, as I will have to decide what to do with it: publish through a traditional publisher (well, try anyway) or publish independently.

I am from a corporate background and spent a lot of time planning in boardrooms. Writing a series of commandments is a form of strategic planning, so it's something I am already comfortable with. I am aware, though, that many people may find this a little strange, but hear me out.

Just like biblical commandments, I can refer to these further down the road if I reach an impasse with my work or feel as though I am veering in the wrong direction. Commandments shouldn't be mistaken for goals. Goals have a determined outcome. You can tick them off when they are complete. These commandments don't work like that. They are more like firm guidelines. If you were trying to steer an enormous ship, following the commandments should help you point the ship in the right direction.

***Thou shalt create a lasting legacy.*** I have already mentioned that as I got older, I looked back over my career and didn't like the idea that most of the projects and products I have worked on no longer exist. With my writing, I want the result to live long into the future after I am gone. This feeling is a symptom of midlife crisis. I never used to worry about such things, but now I do. I want a lasting legacy, something I am proud of that doesn't go out of date or expire.

***Thou shalt create something to pass on to thy children and grandchildren.*** Following from the previous commandment, by creating a lasting legacy I am proud of, I can pass my work down to my descendants. If my books ever become a success, this will help my children in the future. Even if the books are not a financial success, long after I have shuffled off this mortal coil, I will still have a body of work that my family can remember me by.

The legacy of my other work in creating online corporate training just wouldn't have the same sentimental impact on my family, even if I think that work is pretty good.

***Thou shalt not prioritise financial gain.*** This is quite an important commandment. Creative writing can either be a passion in which monetary gain isn't the key success factor or I can treat it like a business. I put substantial thought into this—probably too much, considering I haven't finished writing the novel as I write this chapter—but I am an over-thinker.

I have been very fortunate that, for the many years I have worked for myself, I find fun in employment. However, when you do something that is fun but also your job, the shine can eventually wear off as financial-related stress sets in. For my 'day job', a bit of that stress is a given. It's how I earn my living and help provide for my family. So, the question is, do I want creative writing to be a job?

On the one hand, the thought of sitting here writing novels every day sounds fantastic. Who wouldn't want that? But if I have other people and companies depending on the words that I write, would that fun diminish for me? I already know the answer: *Yes*. Having commitments and dependencies can and will lead to stress. Is that what I want with creative writing? I don't think so.

Don't misunderstand that I never want to earn money from my writing. I want people to read my stories, and I would rather they do that by buying them. If that means earning a good income from writing, then that would be fantastic. What I am saying with this commandment is that I am not prioritising financial gain. If I put the books out and they only sell a handful of copies but I am happy with the finished product, I will still consider that a success. If many sales come my way, that is icing on top of this literary cake.

**_Thou shalt produce thy best work_**. While writing a novel, the author is on their own in crafting the story. However, to produce your best work, you need the help of others, such as editors, beta readers and proof-readers. Professionals need to be hired to create book covers that fit the genre and make your book fit in with other books. If I publish the book myself, I will hire all these people to help me make the best book I can. I would follow the same steps that a traditional publisher would follow. I don't intend to take any shortcuts. I would have to pay for these services, and they can be quite expensive, but people spend money on their hobbies and interests all the time. Writing and publishing a novel is no different.

**_Thou shalt seek to satisfy thy vision above that of anyone else_**. In traditional publishing, there is constant talk about writing to fit market trends. A good example is how the _Hunger Games_ series created a resurgence in dystopian young adult books. With the success of the _Hunger Games_, publishers started looking for young adult dystopian stories, and the market became flooded. If you queried for an agent and publishing deal at just the right time with a book that fit the dystopian trend, you had a better chance at a deal. However, over time, young adult dystopian books fell out of favour. It's not that they are bad, but the market cooled to them and other genres became the 'in' thing.

You may have written an amazing dystopian adult book, but if that's not what the publishers are looking for at this moment, you may face a barrage of rejections. On the one hand, I get it. The publishers are businesses with enormous overheads; they must publish what's trending to make money. On the other hand, this means that the selection doesn't feel fair to the creative who has spent months, if not years, slaving over their book.

The novel I am writing, *Diary of a Martian* (more on this later in the book), is a science fiction book, aimed at a middle-grade level audience. I am writing the book because I think it's a fun story and I like the characters. In terms of market fit, I am not sure how well it would do with a traditional publisher. At the time of writing, fantasy books for a middle-grade audiences seem to be doing well, but with a science fiction theme, I am not so sure. My book is presented as a diary of the main character and the influence I draw on is from the *Diary of a Wimpy Kid* series, even though the tone of my book is very different to the Wimpy Kid books.

If I were thinking with a commercial mindset, I might be tempted to abandon the book and work on something else with more commercial appeal. If I did that, it might take me a year to eighteen months to write the book, at which point the market may have moved on again to something else and all that effort would have been wasted.

If I ignore the commercial and market-focused aspects, I can just write the book I want to write because I want to write it. This may not be the best business approach, but I have already decided that this is a creative exploit and financial gain isn't my key priority. If the book sells well, fantastic. I would love that. But I am not treating creative writing as a get-rich scheme.

**Thou shalt not sacrifice thy rights on the altar of success**. I am fortunate in that I have been traditionally published before for nonfiction books, so I know what that environment is like. I am also now friends with people who have traditionally published fiction. Signing that publishing contract can be exciting, and if that is what you want, you should go for it.

However, there is a side to it I don't like. When you sign that publishing contract, you are signing away the publishing rights to your work. A standard length of this rights transfer is the lifetime of the author plus seventy years, unless you specifically sign for a shorter timeframe. You still own the copyright, but you are giving away the rights to publication. If your book sells, and you go through multiple reprints, you are in an excellent position. The harsh truth is, though, that most books do not earn enough money to cover their advances and make any additional money for the author. If you get an advance, it is just that: an advance on future earnings. The publisher wants that money back before you see any royalties, and most royalty rates for traditionally published books are very low—between ten and fifteen percent.

If your first print takes a long time to sell, the publisher may decide that your book is not viable to pay for another print run, and the book will go out of print. If that happens, there is nothing you can do about it. You don't own the publishing rights anymore; the publisher does, so you are at their mercy. Your contract may have a clause stating that, if sales dip below a certain threshold, you may discuss regaining your rights. Sounds good, but there is a catch.

The publisher can still sell a digital version of your book. I have spoken to authors who wanted to regain their rights based on sales volume, but the publisher set the eBooks temporarily to 99p (or 99¢ in the United States) and ran a promotion for a month. At this price, a lot of copies sold and the book was then returned to its normal price. The publisher hit the sales threshold to keep the rights.

Many writers are happy to agree to these terms as they are desperate to be published by a traditional publisher, but for me, the sacrifice is too great. I don't like the idea of signing away the publication rights to a story that I spent a long time writing. I am not prepared to give away the rights to my work. I would rather sell fewer copies but retain all my rights than take a gamble that a publisher will sell more copies than I can on my own.

The traditional publishing industry looks very different than it did ten years ago. As an author, you are initially on your own to promote your book. If your book gets some traction and sells well, the publisher will start advertising and promoting your work. Until then, they expect you to promote your own book—all for a small royalty percentage. Social media marketing is expensive as you pay per click. The minimal royalty rates on offer from a traditional publisher make any form of paid advertising too expensive to see a reasonable return. If you publish the book yourself, then you earn a much larger percentage of each copy sold, which makes paid social media marketing a better and more worthwhile deal.

## Key Takeaways

Having a sense of meaning in our lives is crucial, both in terms of creativity and for the sanity of the people who surround us. Until my mid-forties, I didn't realise that most things I held dear from my career and the projects I worked on no longer existed. They were a piece of history destined to fade from memory as the years went on. I never used to worry about that, but now I do. While grappling with this creative void, I had a lightbulb moment that writing is a medium that outlives its creator. As thriller novelist Lee Child said, 'When you die, your story still lives'.

I don't mean to say that anything you do in life that doesn't have longevity is bad and has no meaning. I have enjoyed everything that I have built and worked on throughout my career. But if you want to put effort into something that can live on, either commercial or sentimental, then creative writing is a fantastic endeavour. Good food for thought.

In this chapter, I focused on my personal writing commandments. The commandments I walked through express my views, which may differ from how you feel. And that's fine! I urge you to think about your own commandments to identify what's important to you. Your writing commandments help you avoid veering off in the wrong direction.

First though, I need to finish writing the novel itself, as, without a novel, all goals and commandments are pointless.

FIVE

## What I am trying to Write

In January 2021, the United Kingdom went into another full-scale COVID-19 lockdown. This lockdown didn't feel as stressful to me, as the schools were better prepared for online learning than in previous lockdowns. With a less stressful lockdown, my mind felt clearer to think up short story ideas.

Towards the end of January, I came up with a story with two characters, a boy called Elliot and a girl called Mei, who live on Mars as fourth-generation Martians. One day, when these children are in class, an alarm sounds and they must evacuate the colony building. It was a pretty action-packed short story. If you are interested, I have included the original short story in the appendix of this book.

Writing this story was fun. I loved the setting on Mars and the characters, Elliot and Mei. This short story spurred another idea: I would write more short stories, but in the same world. Some stories would be with Elliot and Mei and some with other characters. For a few months, my intention was to put together a collection of short stories in this world.

As I planned out my stories—more on that later in this book

—I evolved what looked like a story arc for Elliot and Mei. It didn't take much more planning for me to realise I had the start of a potential novel instead of a short story collection. Considering our lockdown situation, I became quite excited about the idea.

To start my planning process, I came up with a 25-word pitch to set the feel of the novel.

> *When Martian colonists discover a doorway in a hidden tunnel, humanity can finally answer one of its biggest questions: Are we alone in the universe?*

This simple pitch, or log line, helped solidify the premise I had when planning the short stories. For the Martian setting, I had the idea of two colonies: one called New London, a part of the Global Space Alliance, a future NASA-style agency, and one called New Beijing. Both colonies are located around the base of the Olympus Mons volcano on Mars. The colonies are rivals, established by competing space agencies.

At the start of my story idea, the two colonies unite. However, as you can imagine, not everyone is happy about the idea, which raises the threat level at the start of the book.

My protagonist, Elliot, who is a resident of New London, and Mei, a resident of New Beijing, soon become good friends. Elliot is my main character—I based him on my son, Daniel—and Mei is his friend in the story. While this is Elliot's story, Mei is essential to the plot. Armed with my basic premise and details about my characters, I started some market research. I know that in the previous chapter I said I would not write to market, and I stand by that. I was going to write this book, regardless. Still, I wanted to look at what was already out in the market to make sure I targeted the right audience.

## Genre and Market Research

I already knew that I wanted to target the middle-grade reading age, which is nine to twelve years old. This is the reading group I had been writing my short stories for. What I needed to think about was how long a book like this would need to be and what sort of story structure it should have. From my research, I knew that for middle-grade book publishing, word count was important, so I looked at books on the market to see how long they were.

If the authors were already famous, I looked at their first few books, written when they were unpublished or lesser known. Middle-grade falls into two major categories: lower middle-grade and upper middle-grade. Lower middle-grade books are easier reads of about thirty to 40,000 words. Books by David Williams and Roald Dahl are good examples of this category. Upper middle-grade books tend to have 50,000–80,000 words. Books like Artemis Fowl and the early Harry Potter books are good examples.

I wanted a more accurate idea of the range, so I needed some average word counts. If you search for a book on the kobo.com store, a vendor of eBooks, the sales page for a book will tell you the word count, which is very helpful. Here are some example word counts for books in the area I wanted to write in.

*Harry Potter - Philosopher's Stone* (J. K. Rowling) – 80,000
*Harry Potter - Chamber of Secrets* (J. K. Rowling) – 89,000
*Artemis Fowl* (Eoin Colfer) – 61,000
*Artemis Fowl: The Arctic Incident* (Eoin Colfer) – 61,000
*Sky Thieves* (Dan Walker) – 58,000
*Desert Thieves* (Dan Walker) – 60,000

*Light Hunters* (Dan Walker) – 61,000
*Percy Jackson* (Rick Riordan) – 90,000
*The Secret Diary of Adrian Mole* (Sue Townsend) – 57,000

I have read all these books and consider them to target the audience I want to write for. What I gleaned from this exercise is that a range of 50,000 words on the lower end to 80,000 on the upper end seemed reasonable. If I were to split the difference, my actual target would be 60,000–70,000. This gives me a rough idea of the amount of writing I will need to do.

On looking into word counts in more detail in articles and videos from agents, I learned that for a middle-grade debut, the word count agents generally look for anywhere from 40,000–65,000 words, with the longer word count reserved for science fiction/fantasy books that require heavy world-building. So, my initial estimates were not too far off. You can easily push these word counts a little if you decide to publish independently, but going too high might put off all but the most advanced readers in the target age category.

Doing this sort of research up front before even knowing what the book is going to be about may seem strange. Many writers like to start with only a basic premise and a rough idea of a character, but, perhaps because of my background in software engineering, I am the sort of person who likes to plan.

I will talk about writing from the seat of your pants and planning a little later because, as I wrote, my thoughts on the subject changed unexpectedly. How's that for some foreshadowing and a cliff-hanger?

## Book Goals and Style Guide

As someone who likes to plan, I set myself goals for the book, along with a style guide. I find making some stylistic decisions in advance helps establish a series of guard rails, so I don't veer off target. I have done something like this for pretty much every project I have worked on in my professional career.

***Middle-grade reading age***: I set out to target a reading age of nine to twelve years old. While I targeted a younger audience, I would like the book to be fun for adult readers too. As already discussed, middle-grade is split into two areas: upper and lower middle-grade. Lower middle-grade is aimed at younger readers and has a word count of fewer than 40,000 words. These are short, easy-to-read, fun books. Upper middle-grade books are aimed at a more advanced reader in the same age group and can be 60,000–75,000 words long. These are challenging but fun stories that children and adults, alike, can enjoy.

***Chapters presented like diary entries***: The book is called *Diary of a Martian*, as I wanted the chapters to be presented as diary entries written by the protagonist, Elliot. Therefore, the book would be written in the first person and past tense, and each chapter would take place on a particular date. However, I wanted the chapters to read as flowing prose rather than a rough, realistic diary entry. The book is very much about the world seen through Elliot's eyes.

. . .

***Minimal description of the main protagonists***: I remember reading in a few books and in some writing craft videos that, with children's books, it can be a good idea not to describe the protagonists in too much detail, as children like to imagine themselves in the role of the main character. After putting some thought into that idea, I agreed and applied it in my novel. For example, I don't describe Elliot's appearance. We know he is a boy of average height for his age (twelve years old). I don't describe eye or hair colour, or any other relevant descriptive details, unless required for the plot.

With my secondary protagonist, Mei, all I describe is that she is Chinese and has shoulder-length black hair; I believe that is enough detail for the reader's imagination. The fact that she is Chinese is important to the plot, as I show the two previous rival Martian colonies coming together.

I hope that both boys and girls who can imagine themselves in these roles will enjoy the novel. I know that under-describing characters can be controversial and there are strong opinions on it, but for me, I feel this is right for the story. My secondary characters are described in more detail. When I reach the editing and revision stage of the manuscript, I may change my mind when I read the story back in its entirety. The level of character description I use will be a topic I revisit a few times.

***Short chapters for a fast-paced read***: To make the book an easy read for younger and reluctant readers, I want to keep the chapters short: around 1200–2000 words. Those limits are not a hard and fast rule, but more of a guideline. I want to create fast-paced, forward momentum for the reader.

Many younger readers—and I am basing part of this on my own children—read at night before bed. In my household, we have made it a habit that at 7 p.m., the children must read. This means they have around thirty minutes to an hour to read before lights out. I want the completion of a chapter to feel like a win for the child, so they feel encouraged to continue. If you complete a chapter that is short, you feel more compelled to read the next chapter, especially if there is a cliff hanger to entice you to turn the page.

I read many books on the Kindle e-reader, which tells me how long I have left in a chapter based on my reading speed. If I am reading a book and the e-reader tells me the chapter is fifteen minutes or shorter, I am more inclined to read it. When I complete that chapter, if the Kindle tells me the next chapter is only ten minutes long, I will continue. Before I know it, it's 1 a.m.

Other books I have read have very long chapters, so if I complete a chapter and the Kindle tells me the next chapter is forty-five minutes long, I will stop reading and go to sleep because I like to complete a chapter before putting the book down.

This isn't scientific advice. I am basing these observations about chapter length on my reading habits and those of my children, but that's okay with me and it formed the basis of my plan to keep my chapters short and fast-paced.

**Chapter cliff-hangers to encourage forward momentum**: Along with short chapters, I want to have a cliff-hanger at the end of a chapter. I don't want to force myself to do this on every chapter, but if the action is buzzing, ending a chapter when something interesting is about to happen is a great way to encourage the reader to keep going.

Cliff-hangers have been used in TV shows for decades. The main character gets into a dangerous situation, but the episode stops. You have to tune in next week to find out what happens, or let Netflix (or your streaming service of choice) guide you into the next episode. It's a simple and effective technique to ensure audience engagement and I intend to exploit it as much as I can.

***Main characters are twelve years old***: At the start of the book, my protagonist, Elliot, is eleven years old, on the verge of his twelfth birthday. Twelve years old is the top of the middle-grade reading age range. Children like to read up in age rather than down, so a ten-year-old reader would prefer to read about children older than them and not younger. Reading down in age can feel a bit too babyish. I took this advice from R. L. Stine's Masterclass course and talking to my own children confirmed it.

***Rich and visual world-building***: Children are highly visual. In addition to a gripping story line, fast action and likeable characters, they need the setting to be rich and visual. However, a balance must be struck. Because too much description and exposition can put off younger readers, any description included in the story needs to hit its mark straightaway.

I expect this balance will be difficult to get right, so I will rely on beta readers and editors to help me. But my goal is for the children—and adults—reading this novel to imagine a realistic yet rich world in which the story takes place.

## Story Theme

To write an entire novel, your story needs depth to keep it interesting for the reader, even for a younger audience. What I mean by depth is seeing more of the characters world than just the main plot. *Diary of a Martian* has a well-defined plot. The characters go from point 'a' to 'b' and so on until a resolution has been reached, but at the same time, I want the readers to see more of their lives than the main plot requires.

I remember watching a documentary with George Lucas, the creator of *Star Wars*. In that documentary he talked about the plot of the film, but he also said that *Star Wars* was a family drama. We learn just as much about the characters' families and circumstances as we do about the direct plot and action. I wanted to achieve the same goal. Again, this is a balancing act, as I must keep the readers engaged while imagining what it is like living on Mars.

When I started my planning for *Diary of a Martian*, I wanted to ground the story so that the characters and setting feel normal to the reader, even though the story is set far into the future and on a different planet.

One way to achieve this is to anchor the story in something familiar. For that, I used the humble game of football (soccer for my American friends). Football plays a large role in Martian colony life, bringing people together and making the setting feel familiar to its readers.

I also defined several themes I wanted in the story, including the tension around two colonies uniting, loss and handling bullies. I go into more depth on themes later in the book.

## Key Takeaways

I enjoy the process of planning a book. I know some writers hate the idea of planning, but by putting some effort into understanding what you are writing, the genre and the readership, you can go a long way to avoiding writing a book that you need to change or abandon later.

In any project I embark on, I have always liked the idea of putting a series of 'guard rails' in place. These guard rails serve as a set of constraints I need to stay within, so I don't veer off target and produce something that is irrelevant and ill-fitting for my target audience.

These guard rails don't have to be a complete plan of the book. They're just a guide to help keep me moving in the right direction when the writing becomes tougher later on in the project. And it will.

## SIX

## My Writing Tools

In every creative industry, people love talking about the tools they use to create their art. As a former software developer, I was the same. I would meet with other developers to discuss the programming languages we used, the code editors we developed with and all the other cool tools we use day-to-day to help with our jobs.

Writers and novelists are no different. While I am new to novel writing, I am not new to writing and publishing books, and I love discussing tools and techniques as much as the next writer. So, in this chapter, I'll do just that and tell you which tools I use daily and why.

It is worth remembering that writing is one of the few arts that doesn't require many tools or physical equipment/software, which I think is great. You don't need a computer and word processor; you can be just as effective with a notepad and pencil. What you write is just as valid, whether it is on paper or on a screen.

## My Writing Tools

Like many writers, I started out using Microsoft Word for all my writing. It is a good word processor that is packed with features and stable. I had one problem, though: I get intimidated by enormous walls of text, which I know sounds strange when my job as a former software developer is dealing with enormous walls of text. When I was writing one of my nonfiction books, *The Path to Freedom – Starting a Business for the Reluctant Entrepreneur*, I started the book in Microsoft Word. At 150,000 words, the finished book is large. When I was writing the first draft, I became anxious as it increased in size.

To relieve this anxiety, I split the file into separate Word files for each chapter so that each file was no longer than 10,000–15,000 words. This felt much better, and I carried on this way for half the book.

## Scrivener

Out on a walk one day, I was listening to a podcast when an advert from a company called Literature and Latte for a writing product called Scrivener caught my attention. Scrivener is a writing tool aimed at people writing books, whereas Microsoft Word is a general word processor. There is nothing wrong with a general word processor, but Scrivener has some tools that make a writer's life easier.

The key feature I like is that you can split chapters into multiple files when working on them, but Scrivener will still treat those files as one large document when exporting your work. For example, let's say I am working on a nonfiction book. I can have a folder per chapter and even split that chapter into multiple files. What I do is designate 'Heading Level 1' as the root of the chapter, and whenever I introduce a new topic in that chapter that is marked using 'Heading Level 2', I split it into a separate file. This means I am never working with a block of text that is longer than your average blog post. For someone who finds a wall of text intimidating, this simple feature is amazing, as you can break your writing into manageable chunks.

Another feature of Scrivener that I find very helpful is the binder. The binder is the virtual equivalent of a large binder where you store research notes. This means you can collate all your research, story ideas and planning in the binder alongside your draft. If you are familiar with tools like OneNote, Evernote or Apple Notes, then Scrivener works in a way similar to these applications. All the research for my books goes into a folder in Scrivener and the research documents can then be hyperlinked together, making it very easy to find research information while you are drafting. Using the split-screen editor feature, you can arrange your draft on one side of the screen and your research notes or beat sheets in another window.

I also like the snapshot tool. If you are working on a chapter and want to try a risky or disruptive edit, you can take a snapshot of the chapter first and then make your changes. If, for any reason, you don't like the new edits, you can restore the chapter to a previous snapshot, making risky edits safer to write.

Scrivener also has a brilliant set of tools for tracking word counts and daily word goals. I don't use this personally, but I know many writers do, and it helps keep a writer focused on hitting their daily goals and, over time, completing a book.

I am not endorsing Scrivener, but I think it is worth looking at. It is a powerful application. Considering its feature set, its price is reasonable when compared to an application like Microsoft Word or Office 365. I haven't even scratched the surface of its capabilities, but I am trying to learn about new features.

## ProWritingAid

Another tool I rely on daily is an editing tool called ProWriting-Aid. With ProWritingAid, you can paste text into the tool, and it will analyse your writing and suggest ways for you to improve what you have written. There are various template settings you can apply to tailor the advice to the genre of text you are writing. For my nonfiction work, I set this to 'General Nonfiction', while, for *Diary of a Martian*, I set this to 'Children's'.

The best way to think of ProWritingAid is as a turbo-charged spelling and grammar checker, but the advice it gives you runs deep. It will identify any passive statements in your writing and offer advice on fixing them. You will be advised about excessive glue words that need removing and be told where sentences are difficult to read. The level of advice the tool offers is exceptional.

I will cover my editing process later in this book, but once I have made several revisions of a chapter, I always run my text through ProWritingAid before I let anyone see my writing. It catches so many small issues that you can be blind to when you are so close to your work. The tool isn't perfect, and it makes some suggestions that I don't agree with, but that's fine. As the author, you get to decide which changes you apply or ignore.

One feature I like is ProWritingAid's integration with Scrivener. You can load your Scrivener file into ProWritingAid and edit the files in place, which is a huge time saver for me. ProWritingAid also integrates with other tools like Microsoft Word, but it's the Scrivener integration that matters to me.

ProWritingAid is a very advanced tool for helping you edit your work, but it doesn't replace a human editor. ProWritingAid allows you to eliminate all the silly mistakes you should fix yourself before your editor receives the files so they can focus on finding bigger issues. If you are paying a human to edit your work, you don't want them spending all their time resolving small grammar mistakes.

Discovering ProWritingAid was a revelation to me, and it is part of my daily toolkit. I am the sort of writer who likes to do light editing as I go along. I write a chapter, read through it several times and try to fix any glaring problems. I simplify sentences, kill adverbs and so forth. When I have done this, I load that chapter into ProWritingAid and let it make its suggestions. I fix as much as I can. When I have done this, I move on to the next chapter. Even though I have done some light editing, I still expect to make large revisions at the first draft stage. Still, when I am writing, I like to make each chapter as clean as possible before I move on.

Not all writers are like that. Some prefer to just write and worry about editing and corrections later, but I always feel better if I know my previous chapters are clean. Editing as you go, versus writing without looking back, is a personal decision that a writer must make. Just because I like to perform light editing as I go, doesn't mean you have too, but tools like ProWritingAid are fantastic at helping you mould your prose into shape, no matter when you start editing.

In my experience, performing light editing as-you-go means the revision and editing phase at the end of your first draft can feel a little more straight-forward; this has certainly been the case with my nonfiction books. I know some writers who believe in performing no editing until they have a first draft, and all of them have commented that the revision stage is very tough for them as there is more work to do. It doesn't really matter which approach you choose, but I personally like to front-load some of the editing work as I go to make my life a little easier when I revise the finished first draft.

## Other Tools and Options

Just because I use Scrivener and ProWritingAid, doesn't mean you have to. There are many tools on the market, both paid and free. You don't even need a computer. Many writers still write longhand in notebooks. It doesn't matter what you use. The work you produce can be just as effective if you are writing on paper as if you are typing on a computer. I like Scrivener because it lets me break my writing into manageable pieces and keep all my planning and research in one place, but there are many alternatives.

If you have a Microsoft Office subscription, then Word is a popular choice. It is an industry standard. I still use it from time to time. If I need to send work to an editor, most require it to be in Microsoft Word format, so I export from Scrivener to Word and send that file.

If you are an Apple Mac user, you can use Word, but the Mac also comes with a very good word processor called Pages. Pages is free, so if you have a Mac or iPad, you already have the tools you need, right out of the box.

If you like the idea of using open-source software, you might consider applications like LibreOffice and LibreWriter. LibreWriter is an open-source alternative to Microsoft Word, and it is very good. If you don't want to purchase a word processor, then it is a great option.

If you like the idea of using something that's on the cloud, Google Docs is an obvious choice. Google Docs is an online-hosted equivalent to Microsoft Office that is free to use. It is very popular in businesses as an Office alternative, and I know quite a few writers who use it to write books.

## Key Takeaways

The tools you choose to use are very personal to you as a writer. Everyone has different preferences, but the choice of tool doesn't matter. What matters the most are the ideas you have for your story and your motivation for putting those ideas down on paper or the computer.

Use what works for you, and don't feel as though you must spend money on writing software. There are plenty of free alternatives to the paid options.

## SEVEN

# Jumping on the Learning Train

When I became more serious about creative writing during the Covid-19 lockdowns, I decided I wanted to learn the craft as best I could. I am the sort of person who needs to learn everything I can about a subject. I've always been like that. I can never go into something half-hearted. First, I ordered some books, which I read. I also had a LinkedIn Learning subscription, so I found courses there to watch; I started searching for channels on YouTube, as well.

Learning about a subject such as creative writing can be just as fun as the writing itself. I dutifully read my books and watched online courses in the evening whenever I had a little spare time, drinking in the information as best I could. Learning is exciting and motivating, but it also gave me something to focus on during the COVID-19 lockdowns and home-schooling.

Early on, I decided that I would not tackle a novel straight-away, so I began writing short stories. A few of the books I ordered were about short story writing. Short stories seemed like the ideal projects to be working on at the time, as they allowed me to try different techniques and were small, self-contained projects that could be completed quicker than an entire novel.

In January 2021, when the United Kingdom entered another national lockdown, I was working from home, and I had an idea for a short story set on Mars—the airlock escape story mentioned earlier that you can find in the appendix of this book. I enjoyed writing all my short stories, but it was this story set on Mars that got me excited.

As I said in an earlier Chapter, my initial intention was to write a short story collection, with each story based in the same Martian colony and using the same characters. I was quite excited about this idea and started planning the stories. (If you haven't figured it out by now, I'm a planner—more on that in the next chapter.) What I found was that I had many recurring characters and some stories that felt like they could form the basis of a larger plot. Perhaps this wasn't a short story collection, but an idea for a larger novel. I knew the story was going to be middle-grade level, so I bought piles of books in the target reading age and started working my way through them. This was a lot of fun, but also formed a part of my learning process. In reading the books, I wasn't checking out the competition as much as looking at how to pitch the plot and bring the story to life.

I wrote a basic plot synopsis quite quickly, but I was hesitant to jump straight in and start writing. Part of that stemmed from a fear of screwing up the story and losing interest. Part was procrastination. To make the book as good as possible, I decided I would like to take a writing class—an actual class, not just online videos. I had two options: sign up for a creative writing degree programme or find a commercial class.

Friends with degrees in English literature told me that taking a degree was not worth it for me. You will end up reading books you hate, the courses rarely focus on creative writing on its own and it is unlikely that a published author will teach you. They had good points. English literature degrees are largely about reading and interpreting passages from books and, knowing my luck, the reading would be a lot of literary fiction, which isn't a genre I enjoy.

Every day, I like going out for a walk. During the lockdowns, it was the only thing you could do to get out of the house. When walking, I would listen to podcasts. My favourite show is called the Writer's Routine. The host interviews different writers and talks about their books and their writing process. It's a bit like those behind-the-scenes documentaries that you get for movies.

Some episodes were sponsored by a training company called Faber Academy. Faber Academy is associated with the publisher Faber and Faber. On hearing the advert—yep, sometimes marketing works on me—I checked them out and liked what I saw. They have a particular course called 'Write a Novel' that you can either take in-person or online, though the in-person version wasn't running because of the pandemic.

The online course was quite expensive at over £2000, but it seemed to tick all the boxes in terms of what I was looking for. It was a structured course that was part learning and writing assignments and part committing to word counts for your own novel. Your classmates would critique the words you write towards your novel. To me, this was the most valuable part of the course. Looking at the course structure, it didn't teach you anything that you couldn't learn from a book, but the commitment to word count and peer critique drew me in.

If you just completed the minimal word count on your novel, you would have 15,000 words written by the end of the course. A professional, best-selling author would then assess and critique those 15,000 words at the end of the course.

It wasn't an immediate decision to apply; I spent several months thinking about it. I didn't want to commit to completing the course. After all, there was a high probability that we would still be in a lockdown and that the schools would be closed, which would make it difficult for me to do the required work. In the meantime, I carried on working on my story plan and writing short stories.

In June 2021, I applied for the course. Admission wasn't guaranteed; you had to apply and complete some writing tasks first. The first assignment was a writing sample. This was easy enough. I submitted one of my short stories. Another task was to write a brief plot synopsis of the book you wanted to write as part of the course. That didn't take long, as I had already been working on this.

The final assignment was a short piece about a book that contributed to you wanting to take the course and write a novel. I chose the children's retelling of Homer's *The Odyssey* and *The Iliad* by Gillian Cross. My justification was that this book did a brilliant job of retelling a complex story and writing it in a way that children could enjoy.

I submitted my application at the end of June 2021 and then had a long, agonising wait to see if I had been accepted. There were a couple of options for the course: an online class via a portal website and zoom calls, or an in-person class. The in-person class would require travelling to London every few weeks to the Faber and Faber offices. While that sounded fun, the in-person course was more expensive and would also require travel and hotel expenses. Also, I couldn't rule out COVID-19 closing the in-person classes.

The course intake I applied for was due to start in September. A few weeks before classes started, I received an email from Faber Academy. I had been accepted! I paid the course fee and waited for it to start.

The course was excellent. I got a lot out of it. While many of the topics were nothing new and could be found in any novel writing manual, the exercises each session, coupled with the accountability of hitting your word count, were just what I needed. I was so motivated that I started exceeding the word count. By the time the course finished in May 2022, I had written 47,000 words: two-thirds of my planned word count.

For me, the most useful part of the course was meeting writers who were in the same position as I: wannabe novelists. We all helped each other and critiqued each other's work. Some of the feedback I received helped me tune my story. Unfortunately, the feedback only applied to the first 15,000 words, but, with the lessons I learnt, I honed my writing style.

## Key Takeaways

For me, learning about creative writing is just as fun as the writing process itself. Whenever you start something new, such as a new hobby, you have a brief window at the beginning when you are motivated to learn as much as possible about a subject. This was the case for me, and I devoured books and online training materials.

While all this was fun, what aided me most was taking an actual writing course that allowed me to work with other people. The act of collaboration and critique with other writers was very motivating and helped me learn about my craft. The Faber Academy course was quite expensive, but there are many lower-cost writing workshops you can take. I found working with other writers just as valuable as learning the physical craft of writing. I should point out that there are also ways of joining critique groups for free through Twitter and other social media platforms. Often public libraries will also have such critique groups, as well.

EIGHT

## Story Planning

It is broadly accepted that there are two types of writers: the 'pantser' and the 'plotter'—or, as George R. R. Martin calls them, 'gardeners' and 'architects'. Writers generally fall into one of these two categories, although it is more like a spectrum than a black-and-white distinction. I thought I was on one end of the spectrum when I started writing my novel, but I soon realised I was more comfortable nearer the other end.

A pantser is a writer who writes by the seat of their pants. When they start their novel, they may have an idea for some characters and a general situation, but apart from that, they don't know where the story will go. They write and make it up as they go along, letting the story develop organically.

A plotter is a writer who likes to know their characters first and has a clear plan for the plot. Before they write, they know the main plot points. Nothing is left to chance, as the work of identifying the plot points and character development is all front-loaded in the writing process.

There is no right or wrong way of tackling a novel. Pantsing your story is just as valid as thorough planning. One famous pantser is the horror and suspense novelist Stephen King, who has often talked about how he starts a novel with a basic premise and an idea of the main characters, but lets the story develop as he writes. As a fan of Stephen King's books, I can say that this approach seems to work very well for him.

At the plotting end of the spectrum, we find the popular writer of legal thrillers John Grisham, who plans his novels in detail before writing. Grisham has said that the more time he spends plotting, the easier his books are to write.

While Stephen King and John Grisham sit on either end of this spectrum, writers don't have to be either/or. J. K. Rowling, for example, took a middle position for the Harry Potter series, using a basic beat sheet to plan where her stories were heading, but filling in details through discovery along the way. This process is sometimes called plantsing: a hybrid of plotting and pantsing.

A beat sheet is a simple document that outlines your entire story from the first scene to the end of the book. By listing out the key plot points, you make your writing process easier. A beat sheet doesn't need to be chapter based, but it lists out the main events that happen in the story to move the plot forward. It is best to think of it as rough guide to keep your writing on track.

Coming from a software development, project management and leadership background, I am no stranger to planning. For most of my career, I have been working in large software development teams, where planning is a mainstay of success. This includes planning from a corporate strategic level to granular fortnightly sprint planning for a team of software development staff. When I started writing *Diary of a Martian*, I knew I was going to be a planner. I didn't even question it.

I found the idea of pantsing a novel terrifying. If I allowed myself to write with no idea of where the story was going, surely, I would run off the rails, and before I knew it, I would have a 250,000-word convoluted mess. Chronic overwriting can be a side effect of pantsing, which means you have an enormous job ahead of you in the editing and revision stage.

My views on plotting versus pantsing changed as I wrote *Diary of a Martian*, though. My initial idea was to plan all my chapters. I even had a template that I used for each beat.

I started Act One by creating a chapter-by-chapter breakdown, using the template below. A lot of stories, including films, break their stories down into the three-act structure. The first act contains an inciting incident that sends your protagonist off on their adventure. Act Two contains rising and lowering action as the protagonist faces obstacles and challenges, stopping them from reaching their goals. Act Three contains the finale of the story and all your plot points should be resolved, unless some of them bleed over into a sequel.

The template would tell me the chapter name, the synopsis, where the tension exists, the chapter's emotional theme/core, the world-building elements to use and the cliff-hanger. To be honest, at the start of writing my novel, I thought I was a novel-planning genius.

**1.1 - Chapter Name**
*Synopsis*: What happens in this beat or chapter.
*Tension*: What creates the tension?
*Emotional Theme*: What emotional theme do I want to convey?
*World-Building*: What world-building elements do I want to include?
*Cliff-hanger*: What cliff-hanger will I leave the chapter on?

I was happy with this way of planning when I was early in the first act; it seemed to work for me. A problem was brewing, though. I started finding this level of planning a little stressful. The more detailed my story became, the more I would question my plan and stress about the story. Part of the fun drained away as I strained to fill in the template. My genius planning idea was getting in the way of my actual writing. Early in my drafting, I also had an idea for another character that seemed to appear out of nowhere. I loved the character and saw their potential, but introducing them into the story would mean veering away from the plan.

During the Faber Academy course, one task was to write a basic beat sheet for our novel. Each beat could be only one or two sentences—nothing more. The task was enlightening. It allowed me to plan the story beats so I knew where I was heading and whether the fundamental premise of the story would hold together. In that task, unlike in my previous template filling, I didn't go into so much detail that it made me stressed.

With my previous method of working from a planning template, a mistake I'd made was trying to plan chapter by chapter; the difference with this task was that I was now planning beat by beat, which felt more liberating. A plot beat doesn't necessarily equate to a chapter. One plot beat could span multiple chapters, if necessary. Below you can see the first two beats from my beat sheet.

**Opening ceremony between New London and New Beijing results in a protest.** Elliot and his class go to the opening ceremony for the Mars Express Transit System that joins the New London colony to New Beijing.

**Elliot spots someone suspicious who can't be identified by Watson (his personal AI).** After an accident in a football game, Elliot's AI chip becomes dislodged, so he must go to the infirmary to get it repaired. On the way, he sees someone behaving strangely.

Planning out the story beats, but not including much detail, enabled me to ensure that my story idea worked throughout the major acts but still left me lots of room for discovery while writing, which is the fun bit. This means that I am not a hard plotter or pantser. Instead, my technique is more akin to J. K. Rowling's plantsing: basic mapping out of the story but still pantsing, to a degree.

As I write this chapter, I have just completed the second act of my first draft, and this plantsing technique has stuck with me through twenty-three chapters. I must admit that I have surprised myself. At the start of my draft, I was convinced that I was a dedicated plotter and planner. I was going to plan my novel to an extreme level, as this is what I have done throughout my career. It turns out I like to live a little dangerously and make up parts of the story as I go along—though, of course, I have my basic beat sheet as a guardrail to keep me on track.

When I was trying to plan my plot beats, I would fill in basic character and location profile sheets to define all the information about character and location before I started writing. But I didn't enjoy the process and completing the character and location profiles added to my general level of anxiety. After switching my planning style from full planning to a hybrid of planning and pantsing, I also relaxed my insistence on filling in the profile sheets.

Now I fill the sheets in as I go along. If I introduce a new character or location, I draft the chapter first, work on it to a point where I am happy and then make basic notes in the character and location profile sheets based on the chapter I have just drafted. Filling in the profile retroactively gives me an easy reference to look back at later in the drafting process. If my main character returns to a location that I haven't written for a while, I can immediately check the details I will need, such as what the place looks like. The details I put into the profiles are basic notes. I am not writing multiple paragraphs. They are just enough to be useful only to me.

I have good intentions of going back over these profiles when I have finished *Diary of a Martian* and expanding the notes to make them easier to refer to in the future. If all goes well, my plan is for *Diary of a Martian* to be a trilogy. When I tackle another book in that trilogy, which could be multiple months after the first book is complete, having detailed notes will help me get started on that new book.

## Character Planning

A novel is much more than just its plot. A good story needs characters and effective world-building. World-building draws the reader into the setting and immerses them, while the characters provide the story's emotional core. In most cases, you should have protagonists that readers care about and antagonists who are overcome and get what's coming to them—or not, if you want the antagonist to win.

*Diary of a Martian* is no different from most other stories, in that a cast of main characters and secondary characters populates its story world. As *Diary of a Martian* is a middle-grade novel, my main characters are children. As twelve years old is the upper reading age for a middle-grade book, I set my characters at that age because children prefer to read up in age and not about characters younger than themselves.

As I started defining my beat sheet for the plot, I also had to think about how I wanted my characters to develop over the story and what problems they could overcome. The protagonist is a boy called Elliot, who lives in the New London colony on Mars. The main secondary character is a girl called Mei, who lives in the New Beijing colony. Early in the story, the two colonies are in the process of integrating and working together. As part of this integration, Mei goes into Elliot's class on a school exchange programme, where they become good friends. I deliberately picked a boy and girl as main characters, as I would like readers of both genders to enjoy the story. A similar approach worked very effectively in the Harry Potter series with Harry and Hermione, as well as in the Artemis Fowl series with Artemis and the fairy LepRecon officer Holly. Having both male and female main characters can help a book appeal to everyone.

My third main character is Dimitri, a school bully who is a complete nuisance to Elliot. When I planned my initial beat sheet, Dimitri didn't exist. He never occurred to me. It wasn't until I started writing the first chapter, where Elliot is at football practice, that an interaction emerged between him and Dimitri that I enjoyed. Suddenly, Dimitri became a much larger part of the story.

Before I move on to talk about world building, here are some notes about my main characters that served as my starting point.

. . .

***Elliot Taylor***: Elliot's mother was killed in an accident two years before the story starts, which means his dad is a single parent. The situation around his mother's death becomes important later in the story, but Elliot is struggling to come to terms with losing her, as any child would. Elliot is also bored. Mars is a restrictive environment. You can't just go outside to play; the environment is very dangerous. Elliot feels hemmed in. He loves Earth pop culture and dreams of visiting Earth, even though he knows that will never happen. Elliot dreams of being a professional writer or journalist, but in the colony, children typically follow in their parents' footsteps when they start their apprenticeships, which Elliot is not thrilled about.

***Mei Ling***: Mei lives in the New Beijing colony. For many years, New Beijing has been a rival to New London, where Elliot lives, but the colonies are now integrating and working together. Mei struggles with life in New Beijing as she struggles with school life and bullies and feels hemmed into her way of life. Like Elliot, Mei only has one parent—Mars really is a dangerous place for parents. Mei doesn't have many friends, so when she meets Elliot, a great friendship blossoms.

When discussing the story with friends and other writers, they often ask me if Elliot and Mei will ever get together romantically. I don't know why, but it always seems to be people's first question. I can say now, definitively, that the answer is no. They will always be in the friend-zone. I see their relationship as more like that of a brother and sister. I think it could ruin the dynamic between my main characters if they ever became attracted to each other.

Developing Mei's personality has been fun. When she is in

New Beijing, her personality is slightly subdued as she tries to stay out of the way of bullies, but when she is with Elliot in New London, she comes out of her shell and is a little wild.

Although I am enjoying building Mei's personality, her struggle/journey was not as well defined when I started writing the novel. I know that in the revision stage, I will have to pay special attention to her development. She is a wonderful character, but I don't want her to come across as simply a plot device. I have work to do.

**Dimitri Petrov**: Dimitri is the third main character in the story. He is the class bully and seems to have it in for Elliot. For a large part of the book, the reader will not like Dimitri much. As the story develops, the reader will see why Dimitri is the way he is and, I hope, empathise with him, as Elliot does.

The more I write Dimitri's character, the more I like him. He undergoes a huge change by the end of the story. I'm treating his arc as a redemption story, as he must make an enormous sacrifice.

Dimitri emerged from my hybrid approach between pantsing and plotting and demonstrates what I like about this approach. When I first started planning *Diary of a Martian*, he didn't exist. He came about by accident as I wrote the opening scenes, and the more time I spent with him, the more I liked him until I promoted him to a main character.

## World-Building

One of my favourite aspects of writing my first novel has been world-building. My story is a science fiction/fantasy story. The story is set on Mars, but far enough into the future that I can take some liberties with the science. The book is not hardcore science fiction, but much of what happens is based on scientific facts that required research.

The colonies on Mars that I portray are quite advanced, established settlements. Elliot is described as a fourth-generation Martian, which means he has Martian parents, grandparents and great-grandparents. For my main character, being born and living on Mars is as normal as being born and living on Earth for us.

When I started planning the world-building aspects of my story, I looked at the current science ambitions to reach Mars. At the time this book is being written, advanced probes are roaming the Martian surface, but a human has never set foot there. Companies like SpaceX (run by Elon Musk) are driven to carry people to the big red planet, and I believe they will succeed. I started by imagining a date when we will have established a basic colony on Mars and sent the first inhabitants with a one-way ticket. I then tried to picture what that future colony might look like. I set my story in the year 2156.

The colony where Elliot lives, New London, is a civilian rather than military colony. Still, the colony is run in a formal, structured manner, which includes observing rank and all the formalities that you would imagine in a structured society. I took this structure as my starting point because Mars is a dangerous environment, so the inhabitants need rules and structure to keep everyone safe.

When describing the colony, buildings and technology, I had fun making up cool tech. The colony is advanced, but I also wanted to have a grubby aesthetic on the buildings. They have been there for a long time and, while structurally sound, the buildings look a little worn in places.

Balancing world-building with storytelling is hard to get right. When I wrote the first chapters, I fell into the trap of over-describing the environment, which led to some info-dumps.

While these were fun to write, I ended up removing them quite early on. Instead, I try to drip-feed world-building information into the story as I go, peppering the action with little details instead of spending a lot of time describing what's in a room.

Often, I have to remind myself that this book is for nine- to twelve-year-olds, so I must factor in shorter attention spans. I don't want the world to feel sparse in my description, but I also can't waste paragraphs on description. I expect this is a balance I will have to return to many times as I finish the first draft and head into the revision process.

While I must be careful about how I describe and interact with the world in the story, my goal is to fire my reader's imagination. Mars is a fascinating environment. As a species, we will colonise the planet. I hope that starts in my lifetime, and I am intrigued by what that will look like. *Diary of a Martian*, while a fun story, also gives me a chance to express my vision of what the future could be.

I have tried to portray the world initially as a utopia—a friendly environment. As the story progresses, we see that the Martian world is not perfect and has many problems. This novel isn't a dystopian story, but it also isn't paradise.

## Themes

When planning the novel, I identified several themes I wanted to incorporate into the story. The book isn't just one straight plot line that runs from start to finish. Smaller plot lines and themes are woven into the main story. I had to be careful that I didn't make any of the themes too complex for the target reader and to remind myself that this story—written in the first-person point of view—is seen through the eyes of a twelve-year-old boy. While some themes might seem suited to adults, in this story, we see them through the eyes of a child.

***Principal Theme (Nationalism and Terrorism)***: The novel's primary theme revolves around nationalism, played out in the two colonies, New London and New Beijing, joining forces. As you might expect, not everyone is happy about the idea. When a new transit system opens, connecting the colonies, an attack on the station causes chaos. One terrorist group will stop at nothing to undermine the joining and close collaboration of these two colonies. Later in the book, when the first contact is made with an alien race, the same group plots an attack against the aliens, but tries to frame the the New Beijing colony for the attack. This is quite a heavy theme, and I don't want to make the book about politics and terrorism, so I had to put a lot of thought into how these events would look through the eyes of a child when their once-safe world is turned upside down.

In discussions on the writing of middle-grade books, the consensus seems to be that tackling larger, more adult themes is okay—particularly for the upper age range of these books—provided the framing is right for the target readers. *Diary of a Martian* doesn't dive into politics or counterterrorism in the way an adult novel might. Instead, I've approached the topic from the point of view of my main character and his friends and turned it into an action-packed adventure.

***Sub-theme (Grief and Moving On)***: In the story, Elliot lives with his dad. I killed his mum (oh, the power we have as writers) in an accident on an orbiting space station above Mars. A sub-theme in the book is coping with the death of a family member and the eventual moving on. This sounds quite dark, and I have been careful not to make the situation feel depressing, but things like this happen and affect the lives of children.

The story starts nearly two years after the death of Elliot's mum. It becomes apparent in the story that Elliot's dad might be seeing someone else, which I portray in a light and humorous way through a role reversal, of sorts, between Elliot and his dad. His dad is nervous to tell Elliot about the person he's seeing, even though Elliot already suspects something. In the end, Elliot takes on the adult role, saying he wants his dad to be happy and giving his blessing for his dad to move on.

Even though the book is set far in the future on another planet, the people who inhabit the colony still have the same problems and issues that we face here on Earth.

***Sub-theme (Handling a Bully)***: From the opening scenes, we see that Dimitri, the class bully, is a problem for Elliot. Another sub-theme, therefore, tackles how Elliot deals with him. Elliot resolves the situation in part but not rising to his taunts, as well as by helping Dimitri in a climactic scene. I wanted to provide some depth to the bully. He is not a jerk just for the sake of it—he is a product of his dad's behaviours. As I grew to like the character, I wanted him to return in the sequel, so I take Dimitri on a redemption arc and he comes out positively at the end of the story.

## Research

With my basic beat sheet in place, a good sense of my characters and some ideas around world building, I was ready to draft the story. Still, I needed to do some research around Mars to ensure my world-building felt as realistic as possible, considering I have never been to nor will I go to Mars.

While I wanted a level of realism in how I portrayed the planet and my fictional colony, the novel is not a textbook or hard science fiction, so I didn't need to go into a lot of detail. Still, I wanted the detail I did include to be convincing.

The main book that influenced me was *The Case for Mars – The Plan to Settle the Red Planet and Why We Must* by Dr Robert Zubrin. In it, Dr Zubrin presents a valid plan for how humanity can reach Mars and create a settlement in a cost-effective (for space travel) way. Most of the detail I desired came from that book, a Mars atlas, various YouTube videos and some documentaries.

The research process was fun (who doesn't enjoy reading about distant planets?), but I had to make sure the research didn't become a distraction from the actual writing. While reading these books, I started writing the first draft. If I came across a detail that I realised was incorrect in the draft, I would jump back and fix the problem.

## Key Takeaways

When you are working out your own writing and planning process, it's useful to experiment. You don't have to settle on the first technique you try. If you think you will be a planner and outliner but you find the planning process stressful, try writing a basic beat sheet and discovering the rest as you write.

If you start out thinking you're a pantser but get stuck and can't figure how to progress the story, try outlining and planning your story—again with a beat sheet. It is okay to adapt and change as you learn.

For me, having that basic beat sheet in place helped me ensure the story was heading in the right direction and that my characters' motivations were well defined.

## NINE

## Finding the Time to Write

I consider myself very fortunate in that I get to write for a living, be that scripts for training courses or other nonfiction books. Fiction, though, isn't something I have a clear path to earn a living from while I write *Diary of a Martian*. It would be fantastic to earn my living from fiction, but that is a long way off, which means I can't justify spending the whole working day on my novel. Ironically, because I write nonfiction books for a living, I can justify writing this very book you are holding in your hands, but we'll gloss over that fact for the moment.

Like the vast majority of people working on novels, I had to fit that writing time into a busy work and life schedule. I run a business and I have a full personal life with my wife and two children, so I have to grab writing time when I can.

I began the first draft of *Diary of a Martian* by trying to write in two-hour blocks in the evening. That works sometimes, but for me, it's not practical to do every night. Once I have finished my day job, spent time with the kids, made dinner, put the kids to bed ... by 9 p.m., I'm tired.

If I were lucky, I would manage two evening writing sessions a week. Any more than that, and I might have a grumpy wife to contend with. I could wait until my wife has gone to bed, which is around 10 p.m., and stay up to write more. I did that sometimes, but it made me tired the next day. So, while that works occasionally, it's not sustainable.

I am more of a morning person, and I'm better at getting up early than staying up late, so I sometimes set my alarm for 5 a.m. to get an hour or two of writing in before the rest of the house wakes up. The early morning writing sessions work better for me, but again, they aren't sustainable if I do that every day. What I needed was a basic writing routine that would work to add words to the novel and keep the rest of my life in balance.

## Defining a Consistent Routine

I wanted to form a routine that would give me a minimal word count each day. Anything I wrote above that count would be a bonus. I settled on three consistent times I could write: when the kids were having their breakfast, during my lunch break and when the kids were having their dinner. In each of those sessions, I would aim to write 350 words, which is not a lot and very doable. In one day, that is 1,050 words. In a week, that's 5,250 words if I work a five-day week or 7,350 words if I work a seven-day week.

This routine was very easy to stick to and, if I did only that, I would have the first draft written in a short time span. Of course, if I was inspired, I still did the occasional early morning or evening writing session, but, at a minimum, just over a thousand words a day seemed reasonable to fit into a busy work schedule.

My time was a little more chaotic when I was taking the Faber Academy course as I had coursework to complete, but with Wednesdays being my lightest workday, I aimed to complete the coursework that afternoon.

I found this new routine very motivating. I could make gradual progress with a small writing burst. These small steps, even with a busy life schedule, made me feel good about myself and what I was trying to achieve. Some weeks, I would hit only the minimum word count—and that was okay. In other weeks, when the ideas were flowing, I would write much more.

Taking my estimation that my final word count for the novel would be about 80,000 words with a minimal word count of 1,050 words, it would only take seventy-six days to write the first draft. Sounds reasonable. Of course, the process doesn't always work out like that, as you can get stuck or need to do some research, but it's a motivating target to aim for.

## Writing Sprints

Back in my software development days, my colleagues and I used to love reading about productivity hacks. One popular technique is the Pomodoro Technique, devised by a man called Francesco Cirillo. The technique, while simple, gives you a better relationship with time so that you can focus without wasting it. While the technique is very popular in software development, it's also perfect for writers. I use it when I can sit down for a longer stretch of time without interruptions.

The Pomodoro Technique uses a kitchen timer that, as the name suggests (pomodoro means tomato in Italian), looks like a tomato, although you don't need to use a physical timer. This technique forces you to work in set sprint lengths that end with a brief break.

The only rule is that when you are working in a sprint, you must not become distracted, which means that you silence your phone and close your email and your browser. You focus only on the work you are supposed to be completing. Nothing should be so urgent that you can't wait until the sprint is over to deal with it, although, to be fair, I have the phone numbers of my wife and the children's schools set to override the silence settings on my phone in case of family emergencies.

This technique is very simple and can be summarised as follows:

1. Define a task: In my case, write a scene.
2. Set the timer for twenty minutes and focus on that task.
3. Take a five-minute break.
4. Repeat for another twenty-five-minute sprint.
5. After four sprints, take a longer break.

It's simple but works well as a way of forcing you to focus. Still, you need to be strict about not allowing any distractions from the phone, email or web browsing. You can install apps on your laptop that help manage the timing of the sprints and breaks with timers and alarms. Some apps will not let you browse the internet apart from specific websites on an allow-list. Personally, I can struggle to stop myself opening up YouTube, so I use a web-blocking application to help if my will is not strong that day.

When you take your five-minute break, it is important to actually take a break from your writing, ideally by leaving your computer. I like to go and get a drink and go into the kitchen, just to get away from the screen. I also try to avoid checking email or social media, as it is very easy to get dragged into something else that will take longer than the break and eat into valuable writing time.

## Key Takeaways

Finding time to write can be a challenge, especially if your writing is a pastime that isn't your primary source of income. Writing a novel is a huge undertaking. It can seem like an impossible mountain to climb, but, as with all challenges, you can make it feel manageable by breaking down the process into small pieces. Instead of worrying about the entire novel, just focus on a scene at a time.

In a busy life, finding time to work on those scenes can be a problem, but a great start is to consistently grab small pieces of time throughout the day and aim to complete short snippets of your story. As I mentioned, I try to write while my kids are having their breakfast in the morning, a little over lunch and a little in the evening. Even on very busy days, I try to maintain this minimum schedule, because a few hundred words here and there soon add up to a lot of words over the space of a week or a month.

For me, realising this was quite transformational. By grabbing bites of time, I could write my debut novel. It's powerful to realise just how much you can achieve by creating regular habits and protecting those small blocks of time. Imagine what you could achieve if you wrote full time and managed 2,000 words a day. That's over 700,000 words a year!

TEN

## Writers Block

There is one subject that seems to strike fear into all writers. Dare we even mention the name? No, not Voldemort. It is *(whispers)* 'writer's block'. It's okay. You can say it out loud.

I have strong views on writer's block, so I will start off with a controversial statement, but please stay with me.

> *Writer's block is just an excuse to not write. It doesn't exist.*

After reading that, you are probably either nodding your head in agreement or about to throw this book across the room. Please don't though, especially if you are reading on an expensive e-reader.

All writers get stuck. It happens to me all the time, but I don't consider it writer's block. My muse hasn't flown out the window. I am just stuck.

Once, I was stuck near the end of the first act of *Diary of a Martian*. I knew where the characters had to end up, but I couldn't find a convincing way to get them to that point. I had an idea, but it didn't seem very good when I started writing. I needed another idea. I wrestled with the problem for about an hour. Still no joy. I went for a walk to see if the answer would come to me like a bolt of divine inspiration. It didn't. I was stuck.

What to do? I could have pleaded that I had writer's block, shut my laptop and done something else. After all, there's an entire world of YouTube and Netflix that needs watching. But that's silly and not very professional. If you work in a workplace where you are accountable to a boss, you most likely wouldn't go and watch Netflix, or anything like that, but you may browse the web, or go walking around the office looking for conversations with other people, which distracts them from their work.

I am a professional writer. I write for a living. Fiction may be new to me, but I have written numerous nonfiction texts, such as training course scripts. What do I do in these stuck situations? I switch to something else—another writing project. In that moment when I was stuck with *Diary of a Martian*, I had another nonfiction book in the early stages that I was working on, so I carried on with that instead. I had already outlined the next few chapters, and I knew what I needed to write. So, there was no so-called 'writer's block' there; I carried on working on that nonfiction book for another four days solid.

The fourth day was sunny. I left a little earlier than usual to collect my son from school, loaded up a TV show music score on my phone and walked the long way. Just over halfway through the walk, I had an epiphany. The divine lightning bolt of ideas struck me. I wasn't actively thinking about the problem in my novel, but my brain must have been chewing on the problem in my subconscious. I figured out how to solve my plot problem. Was it the music that helped or the walk? I don't know. Why didn't I think of this idea initially? Well, I had been stuck. But now I had the answer. I pulled out my phone, pulled up the voice recorder and made a few audio notes. Satisfied, and with a big grin, I finished the walk and picked up my son from school. That evening, I loaded up my novel in Scrivener and finished writing the first draft for the section that was causing me issues.

I don't consider this situation writer's block. I wasn't blocked from writing anything else; I was just stuck on one particular project. My muse may have been confused, but I gave him something else to do for a while.

But what if I'd become stuck with the nonfiction book at the same time? What would I have done? Well, I have a blog and a list of posts I want to write. I could have worked on one of those. I also have a collection of short stories I have been working on. I have a few other ideas for novels rattling around in my head. I have scripts for the online training courses I produce as part of my business. There is always something to be getting on with. It's still writing.

In summary, professional writers don't get blocked. They become stuck and then do something else temporarily. Amateur writers become stuck, think they are blocked and then procrastinate.

I say, choose the professional mindset, even if you are writing as a hobby. Just work on something else until you become unstuck. Car mechanics don't claim to be blocked when fixing a car and then give up for the day. That's a fast track to being sacked. They get help or fix another car. Plumbers don't get plumber's block. Airline pilots don't get pilot's block—I hope. Other professionals don't claim blocks. They get stuck, try to fix the issue or carry on with something else that needs doing and come back to the problem later.

## Key Takeaways

Writer's block is a subject that each writer has their own relationship with, so you may not agree with my views in this chapter. That's fine. Every writer will become stuck on the story they are writing at some point. It's as inevitable as death and taxes. I think it's a shame, though, when a writer becomes stuck, they stop writing at all.

My key takeaway from this chapter is that I recommend that you, as a writer, have other projects you can work on. These might be blog posts, short stories or even another novel that you can chip away at when you are stuck on your primary project.

When you become stuck and you can't solve the problem, don't fight it. Just step away from it and work on something else. That way, you are still practising your writing skills. When you solve your initial problem, you will not only be able to proceed with that project, but you will also have something else to show for it.

## ELEVEN

## Getting Feedback While You Write

When writing a book, receiving quality constructive feedback is important, but it is also very hard to find. Getting anyone to read anything you write, especially before it's released, can be a struggle.

Asking family and friends is one option, but even if they do read your work, their opinions may not be honest. They're more likely to save your feelings than tell you that your writing is terrible, and their opinions will not be as valuable to you as that of another experienced writer. Plus, they may not want to read anything or even have the time to read it.

In fact, the next time family and friends ask you what you are up to, tell them you are writing a novel, but, as you tell them, look into their eyes. I swear anytime you mention this to people, a glimmer of fear flashes across their faces as they worry you will ask them to read your work. For this reason, I rarely talk about my work with family and friends. I'll mention it when the project is finished, but not while I am working on it.

Working on *Diary of a Martian* as a budding novelist, I wanted quality feedback on my writing, but I knew from the start that obtaining it would be an issue I would need to address. I did receive some feedback from the writing course I mentioned earlier. Part of the course involved writing 1,000 words of your novel in each two-week class session and submitting this work for your peers to read and critique. I found this exercise quite valuable and received some useful feedback, and I hope my classmates found my feedback helpful too.

There was one issue with the feedback, though; it was all very polite. I wasn't expecting anyone to say anything mean about my work, but most of the feedback focused on the positive aspects of my writing rather than any issues. It's always nice to hear friendly comments about your work. It massages the ego. But I also wanted more honest feedback about the parts of my story that didn't work.

Another issue with this course (which was very good, overall) was that if you kept up with the word count requirements for each session, you would have a maximum of 15,000 words critiqued by your peers. At the end of the course, my course tutor, a best-selling young adult author in her own right, would also critique those 15,000 words. My tutor's final report didn't disappoint; she went into significant detail, which was insightful for me and helped shape the rest of the novel. But that feedback was only on the first 15,000 words.

Some overall observations about my writing emerged in that report. First, because my book is targeted at a middle-grade audience, I needed to soften some of my main character's descriptions and thoughts to better pitch to the reader age group. That feedback was very helpful as I could then tweak the tone of the rest of the book.

Another observation from the first 15,000 words was that my main character was living in a world largely dictated by the surrounding adults; it's a colony on the Martian surface. My tutor was worried that my main character, Elliot, was more reactionary to his surroundings and situation than active in his decision-making. This very helpful piece of feedback drove me to grant the main character more agency throughout the book.

My tutor also suggested that I needed to be more direct and upfront about Elliot's struggles in his environment, which is very restrictive and dangerous. The Global Space Alliance (the story's NASA equivalent) has built the entire colony around safety, but this makes life difficult for a twelve-year-old. Elliot can't just go outside to play. While I was alluding to this in my story, my tutor suggested that, for the age group I am targeting, I needed to be more upfront and direct.

Finally, she pointed out that while my world-building was very good, I perhaps had too much of it and could remove some scenes that didn't drive the plot forward. World-building versus propelling the plot is a fine balancing act, particularly as science fiction often requires more world-building, but I had to be mindful of the reader age group.

I was thrilled with the honest feedback in my tutor's report. My tutor loved what I was doing and where the book was going, and she helped steer me in a better direction. That is the power of effective feedback—it motivates you and helps you improve.

Receiving feedback like this is very important, even if that feedback isn't always positive. When you are alone writing a book, it can become very difficult to gauge how well you are doing, especially as you get further along with the project. By receiving feedback from a tutor and best-selling author, it gave me the confidence to know what I was writing was good and also what needed fixing. I found that very encouraging.

Something to remember, though: feedback from anyone is still based on their opinion. Hopefully it's an opinion that comes from experience, but, as the author, remember, it's still your book. If you don't agree with some feedback or suggestions, you don't have to accept them. If you reject all the feedback, you need to take a long look at what you are doing and ask, 'why?' If you reject everything, there is a strong chance that your ego is getting in the way of any feedback you are receiving. If you agree with most of the feedback, but disagree with a few points, then that's fine. You have the ultimate creative authority over your book.

## Professional Critique Partner

The tutor's report didn't come until the end of my course, after ten months. While the feedback from my course peers was helpful, I wanted another professional opinion, particularly as this is my first novel. Yet, not knowing any other fiction writers, I felt my options were limited. So, I experimented. I thought it would be interesting to send a few chapters to a professional editor to see what feedback they offered.

I had used the editing company Scribendi before. The best way of describing them is like an editing agency; you submit work, and based on the word count and your required speed of delivery, they charge you up front for that document and, once you have paid, they assign that work to a suitable editor. I had used Scribendi for other nonfiction projects, so I was already used to working with them.

When the document has been edited, they send you back two files. The first file has all the track changes made by the editor, such as spelling and grammar fixes. That's a very useful document to look through to see what the editor has done to correct any issues. The second document has all those minor fixes approved and you're left with the editor's notes. These notes were very useful as they related to the story: for example, 'I would be interested to know what your main character thinks after what just happened' and 'The imagery here could be expanded on; how about…?' The feedback pointed out flaws in the story, offered advice on what I should do to improve a passage and made suggestions to help, for example, about characterisation and setting.

After submitting these first few chapters to Scribendi, I was keen to know more and I loved the feedback from this editor. When the work was returned to me, I received the editor's code number, so I could request the same person again. You're not allowed to know your editor's real name, which, understandably, stops you from hiring them off the platform. I was thrilled with the feedback I received, so I packaged up another small batch of chapters and sent them off, and again, the feedback was very helpful.

If you look at this from a high level, I was paying a professional to edit my work in batches. But instead of thinking of it as editing, I considered it hiring a professional critique partner who would give me honest feedback on the story while I was writing it. The editor would tell me what was working and what wasn't. As I was hiring a professional editor, I would receive an honest appraisal of the work ... unlike asking my wife to read a chapter, who would say, 'It's great', and send me on my way.

I continued sending chapters to this critique partner throughout the novel writing process and learned a huge amount. I must say, though, that I am not expecting you to do this. That's certainly not my advice. It was expensive, and for this first novel, it has cost more than anyone might consider sensible. Even when I complete the book, I will still need an editor to look at it as a whole, so it wasn't like I was short-cutting the process. For my first novel, however, I treated this chapter-by-chapter editing process as a form of education that allowed me to learn from receiving professional feedback.

Would I do this for my second novel? No, probably not. Next time around, knowing what I know now, I will write the novel, polish the manuscript as much as I can and send it off to an editor, which is the usual process. For this first book, however, I was willing to take the financial hit. As I mentioned, I don't have any expensive hobbies. I am not into cars, bikes, boats or anything like that, so for this first novel, I was prepared to invest. It's no different from investing in a mega expensive set of golf clubs. Well, that's how I'm justifying it to myself.

On the subject of justifying the cost of producing the book, I refer you back to three commandments from the beginning of this book:

- ***Thou shalt create a lasting legacy.***
- ***Thou shalt not prioritise financial gain.***
- ***Thou shalt produce thy best work.***

My chief priority is creating a body of work that I am proud of, my family will be proud of and I can call a lasting legacy. Despite the successes in my career, none of it is anything I want to be remembered for when I eventually move to another plane. My fiction, though? I want it to outlast me and for my family to remember the books. Financial gain isn't my priority, which is why I am prepared to invest more in this first book to make its quality as high as possible. Don't get me wrong; if I could earn a living out of writing fiction, I would be thrilled and grateful. But sometimes, to make a living from a new venture, you need some up-front investment and, by investing a little in a professional critique, I can satisfy that third commandment of producing my best work.

## Dealing with Negative Feedback

I have been a writer for a long time, so I am used to receiving feedback on my work. When publishing through traditional publishers, I would have to work with their internal editors, who would provide feedback, good and bad, on my writing. If you are not used to receiving feedback like this, it can be very scary. Just the thought of opening the files you receive from an editor can leave you feeling nervous and a little sick.

When you work with an editor, as well as receiving the marked-up files with all the comments and corrections, you will also receive a brief report highlighting the general observations on any issues found in your work. If you are nervous about taking the criticism, I recommend initially reading only the summary report and letting that sink in. Then, wait for a day or two to open the actual files, so you can prepare yourself for the feedback.

I will say one thing though: any editor you work with is on your side. They want you to produce the best work you can. Even if some of the feedback feels harsh, remember they are providing it to help you and not to be mean. I have had my fair share of harsh feedback over the years, but I would much rather hear it from my editor and fix the issues before I publish the work than receive negative reviews from my readers.

At the back of this book, in the appendices, I have included a couple of blog posts I wrote many years ago. One is about how to handle criticism and the other is about how to give effective criticism. I wrote those blog posts from the perspective of people in the workplace and not about fiction writing, but I think the advice in them still applies. I hope you find them helpful.

## Key Takeaways

Feedback on your writing is essential to the development of any writer, but taking criticism can be tough. Family members and friends tend not to be reliable critics of your work as they will not want to hurt your feelings. So, unless you know other writers or editors, finding quality feedback can be hard.

For me, I had the benefit of peers in a writing course who would critique my work. While they gave some fantastic feedback and offered useful suggestions, the feedback was only on a small part of my manuscript.

You can, of course, take a more extreme approach, like I did, and hire an editor to act as a critique partner throughout the writing process. For me, this was transformational, as I had a professional offering me excellent advice, which assisted my learning. Obtaining this level of feedback was expensive, but it was a conscious decision that I made for my situation. I don't recommend you do this unless you are willing and able to invest the necessary funds. Alternatively, you could hire an editor to assess your first 5,000–10,000 words, then take that learning and apply it to the rest of your manuscript. That way, you would keep the cost down and still gain a professional critique of a cross-section of your writing.

TWELVE

## Self-Doubt After the Honeymoon Period

I've noticed a pattern on every creative project that I have embarked on in my career. I'm very excited about my idea, make grand plans, am eager to start on my first draft and then …

*Diary of a Martian* was the same. I had the initial idea during one of the COVID-19 lockdowns, and I thought it was brilliant. I still do. I developed the idea in my mind and started planning the characters and plot-lines while I practised writing short stories.

When I began writing the first chapter, I was super-motivated and launched into the writing like a man possessed. Progress was rapid. I liked what I had written, and I hurtled through Act 1 of the story.

Then, I hit Act 2, about thirty percent of the way through the book. The critical voice of doubt started speaking. Was the plot engaging? Were my characters likeable? Was my story as good as comparable stories on the market? Was I wasting my time? That critical voice in my subconscious was not nice. It was a bit of a bully.

I've worked on enough creative projects in writing and other mediums to recognise the signs. For some reason, every project gets tough around the thirty percent stage. Thankfully, I knew what was happening, so I could address the problem head on.

But it's very common for a writer who doesn't recognise the signs to give up at that point. Imagine how crushing that is! You are excited about a project, you feel the fires of creative passion burning inside you and then that self-destructive voice of doubt picks on you from the back of your mind. Slowly, you think you are not worthy and give up.

## Why Does this Happen?

This happens for a few simple reasons. First, the honeymoon period is over. The excitement of the idea and its execution wanes. It doesn't mean the idea is any less good than it originally was, but now you are used to it and, as you get used to an idea, the initial excitement factor drops a few notches. It may not tarnish altogether, but the sheen wears off a little.

Another reason is that about a third of the way into a project, you realise just how much work is involved in writing a book. You have already written a sizeable chunk of it, but all you can see is how much work remains and that can be hard to deal with.

I have been there many times on different projects. The worst instance was a business book I wrote called *The Path to Freedom – Starting a Business for the Reluctant Entrepreneur*. This was a comprehensive book, around 150,000 words. It's the largest writing project I have ever undertaken, and about a third of the way into that book, I struggled when I realised just how much work I had left.

There isn't a straightforward way to overcome this hurdle.

No matter what, you are still going to need to put your bum in a seat and your fingers on a keyboard and use sheer willpower to get you through. But there are lots of tricks you can use to help.

### Tactics to Get through the Slump

The following tips have worked well for me over the years. You don't need to apply all of them all the time, but each can help pull you out of that writing lull as you move out of the honeymoon phase on your book. I don't consider this slump writer's block, which was covered a few chapters back. You're not blocked, or even stuck, about what to write. In fact, often when you hit this slump, you know full well what you need to write. It's just your critical brain trying to sabotage you by making you doubt your initial idea.

**Tactic 1: Write every day**. The first technique is to write just a little every day, so you continue to make some progress. When you are in this honeymoon slump, you are not blocked or stuck but are having a crisis of confidence, coupled with fear over the sheer amount of effort required to finish your novel.

In the chapter on finding time to write, I talked about trying to establish a minimum routine for putting words on the page. If you are in this honeymoon slump, but you try to write, as a minimum, 250 words twice a day, that's 500 words a day. If you do that five days a week, that's 2,500 words a week, which is about 10,000 words a month. As the result of a habit requiring minimal effort, that's a pretty good word count.

If you hit 10,000 words a month, I can guarantee you that the negative thoughts about the level of effort required to complete the book will soon disappear, as you'll see just how much progress you can make. If you doubled that minimum word count each day to 1,000 words, in a month, you can write a quarter of an 80,000-word novel. Writing just a little every day is important because that small amount of effort soon adds up to a significant word count and becomes a powerful motivating factor to drive you forward.

**Tactic 2: Work on something else for a while**. As with writer's block, if your brain doesn't want you to work on your current work-in-progress, work on something else, instead. This could be blog posts, if you have a blog. It could be short story ideas or maybe notes for other novels.

I always recommend working on something else as opposed to doing nothing. It keeps your mind active and ensures you continue to practice your craft. If you decide not to write anything, you may fall into a cycle where doing nothing is easier, which makes it hard to get back into work on your current book.

**Tactic 3: Take regular breaks**. No matter which project you work on, whether it be your current novel or another project, if you try to work on it for eight hours a day, taking no breaks, you're going to struggle and your brain will not thank you.

Sprints, which I discussed earlier in the book, are a very effective writing method as they keep you focused for around twenty minutes just on your work. Then, you have to take a break before starting the next sprint. If you decide you don't want to do sprints, and you try to keep regular hours, make sure you take regular breaks throughout the day. I consider a break as time away from the screen. Get a drink, go in the garden if you have one, pop to the shop, sit in a different room—anything that is away from your computer. Checking your email or social media isn't a break.

Your brain is not a machine, and it will need constant breaks to help keep it focused. The mental exercise of writing is like physical exercise. If you do a lot of walking or running, you'll need to take breaks in between those sessions, otherwise, your body will become fatigued.

**Tactic 4: Get plenty of sleep**. If you don't get enough sleep, your brain will be tired. A lack of sleep will mean that you cannot focus on what you're writing; it can also affect your mood. I have experienced this many times. If I get fewer than seven hours of sleep a night, the next day, I find it very difficult to write anything coherent, and writing feels like a struggle.

I try to maintain a similar routine each day. I go to bed between 10:30 p.m. and 11 p.m. and wake up around 6:30 a.m. If I stick to this routine and get good quality sleep, I am always more alert and motivated to work on writing the next day.

Many factors can affect the quality of your sleep. For one, I never try to write late into the night as my brain becomes too active. When I have worked on a book chapter right up to bedtime, it always takes a long time for my brain to calm down. If I am going to write in the evening, I have a hard stop of 9:30 p.m., at the latest. After that, I always read for at least thirty minutes to an hour before bed. I typically read fiction as that helps relax me before I go to sleep.

**Tactic 5: Remove distractions**. If your brain is trying to sabotage your writing during the honeymoon slump, it will not take much for you to stop writing. You will need just the smallest excuse—be that a notification on your phone or the seductive lure of YouTube and its endless stream of delights.

Regardless of whether you are in the honeymoon slump, reducing distractions in your work area is always a good idea. I keep my phone in my work bag on silent. Only the numbers of my wife and children's school can override the silent settings. Apart from that, I keep my phone and iPad out of the way.

On my work computer, I also use an application that allows me to block access to certain websites, apps and social media while I am working. You can, of course, override the app if you need to, but it's a hassle to disable it, and it makes you feel guilty for doing so when you are supposed to be working. Many of these internet blocking apps exist, but I use a Mac app called Focus by Jasper Software.

If you don't want to use an app like this, you can just turn off the Wi-Fi on your computer. It has the same effect. Some writers—and I am not one of these—have a separate computer just for writing that has no internet access and contains only their word processor of choice. This is an extreme measure, but it works for some people. I'm a single-laptop kinda guy.

**Tactic 6: A change of scenery**. This is one of my favourite techniques for keeping me motivated to write. I use it all the time, regardless of whether I'm in a writing slump or not. All that's required is to try writing somewhere different every now and then. If you work from home, spend a morning writing in your favourite coffee shop. I like to do this at least once a week for a few hours and I always find this time very productive, thanks to the novelty factor of being somewhere different.

You could also go to your local library. My library has desks that you can book for a few hours at a time. The desks are intended for people who want to use the library to conduct research, but they are also ideal for writers. There is nothing more motivating than trying to write a book while surrounded by books. And I do like the smell of a library.

Your local town may also have a co-working space where you can use a desk for a day, along with small-business owners. Most co-working spaces will have a simple day rate for hiring a desk, so there will be no large financial outlay. You can just use them when you like.

There are plenty of options for you to explore. The main point is to occasionally change your scenery, because if you write in the same room and at the same desk all the time, you can become a little bored with your surroundings.


**Tactic 7: Break the project down further**. Sometimes, when I am writing, I become daunted by the gigantic wall of text on the screen. When my critical brain is already trying to sabotage me, having that wall of text can put me off. I thought I was strange thinking like this, but after speaking with other writers, I've found the wall-of-text fear is quite common.

When I am in this situation, I like to split my chapters into multiple files, so I am only ever looking at a small piece of text at a time. This is one reason I enjoy using Scrivener as my word processor, because you can turn a chapter document, for example, into a folder and then have separate documents sitting inside that chapter that contain only a small block of text. Even though the chapter is split up into multiple digestible blocks of text, Scrivener still treats that chapter as a single file, which I find very helpful. This means that, at any point, I am only working on a block of text about the size of a small blog post—five-hundred to a thousand words.

If you don't want to write because your brain is trying to

stop you, breaking the work down into much smaller units can make it easier to continue without feeling overwhelmed.

**Tactic 8: Take inspiration from other writers**. When I'm in a creative slump, I like to be inspired by other writers. Listening to another writer talk about their craft is fun, educational and, above all, motivational. YouTube is fantastic for this. Yes, I am giving you permission to procrastinate on YouTube, even though one of my other tactics (Tactic 5) is to remove distractions. While this is a distraction, it can be a helpful in increasing your motivation. But be careful. It's very easy to sink into a video-viewing rabbit hole from which it's hard to crawl back out.

To find something to watch, try picking your favourite writer and searching for interviews where they either talk about their books or their writing process. A personal favourite of mine is Stephen King talking about writing.

I am also a big fan of the video training website Masterclass, which has numerous courses by famous writers like Neil Gaiman, Margaret Atwood, R. L. Stine, Dan Brown, James Patterson and many others. I have learned so much from letting them teach me on that website.

**Tactic 9: Try dictation**. Another technique I have become quite fond of is dictating some of my chapters. I am a Mac user, so this feature is built into the Mac's accessibility features, and it is also built into Windows using Cortana (Windows 10 and onwards). Every now and then, I will set up a mic in front of my monitor, put Scrivener into dictation mode and just say what I want to write.

With this technique, you are shortcutting the conversion of

your thoughts into finger movements. Instead, you are going straight from thoughts, via your mouth, to the computer; it is effective because your brain is having to deal with speaking instead of trying to sabotage you with self-doubt. With *Diary of a Martian*, I dictated about a quarter of the book and I enjoyed the process. It does take some getting used to, as you have to speak all your punctuation. So, writing a line of prose will sound like this:

> This time **comma** Varga spoke **full-stop speech mark** You have your younglings serve in your military **question mark speech mark new line**
> **speech mark** We are a civilian colony **comma** not military **full-stop** When our children reach a certain age **comma** they serve in the colony as part of their training **comma speech mark** said Carter **full-stop**

Initially, this felt odd, and my prose contained many errors, but the more you dictate, the more natural it feels. When I write the sequel, I intend to dictate much more of the book—not all of it, though, as I do like typing on a keyboard.

After I have finished dictating a scene, I go over the text and fix up any dictation mistakes. Perhaps dictation is more accurate with an American accent, since Apple is an American company. I think my British accent confuses the computer sometimes as it substitutes some interesting words.

If you are struggling to write as your critical brain is trying to sabotage you, switching to dictation and bypassing the keyboard can be an effective way to get your writing moving again.

. . .

**Tactic 10: Use a different keyboard**. The final technique I use occasionally is to change the style of the keyboard that I type on. This gives me a different tactile feeling when writing. It sounds silly, but it works. On a normal day, I use a pretty standard Apple Magic keyboard. It's small and has keys that feel more like typing on a laptop than a mechanical desktop keyboard and, over the years, I have become very accustomed to working with it. If I don't feel like writing, and some of the other techniques listed in this chapter haven't worked, I swap my computer keyboard out for a different one.

In my case, I switch to a mechanical keyboard that looks like an old typewriter. It's called a *QwerkyWriter* and it's fantastic. It feels like you are typing on an old typewriter, which is ideal if you want to summon your inner Ernest Hemingway. The keyboard even has a carriage return bar that acts like the return key.

However, even with a padded wrist support, I can't use this keyboard for more than a few days before my wrists ache. But to change the tactile feel of my writing when I get into a slump, this keyboard is a treat to unpack and use. While that particular keyboard is a bit of an expensive luxury, you can use any keyboard that is different from your usual one. It doesn't have to be expensive; you are just trying to change the feel of your writing for a short time.

## Key Takeaways

For any writer, the end of the honeymoon period can be quite distressing. That idea you were so excited about suddenly feels mundane, and when you get to the thirty percent point of your manuscript, all you can see is the mountain of work ahead. This is when that annoying critical voice in our heads tries to derail us and, for many writers, it works and they give up.

For every book I have written and published, I have hit the same problem without fail. The good news is that this is only temporary and, if you can push through that short slump using techniques from this chapter, you will succeed. Over time, you will become better at tuning out that critical inner voice and focusing on your creative voice, which is where the quality words flow from.

THIRTEEN

# My Writing Process

If you were to ask twenty writers what their writing process consisted of, you would get twenty different answers. I find that quite exciting, because every writer is different. It also means that you can't write a definitive chapter on writing processes, as there are just too many to consider.

My writing process has developed over the years with my nonfiction books, so I went into writing *Diary of a Martian* with an existing process that has worked well for me.

When you read about writing processes, you will often hear about the vomit draft (or speed drafting), although that is a pretty horrific name. You just write—or spew (yuck)—your words onto the page, without editing or looking back at any of your writing until you reach the end of the book.

I used to like the idea of fast drafting, as it forces you to keep moving forward until you reach the end of the book. But then I ran into a problem. I would start worrying about the quality of what I had written but wasn't 'allowed' to look at, and that worry would slow my progress.

Worrying about the quality of what I had written took the

fun out of the writing process for me, so I had to adapt. What I changed to, and what I still do to this day, including with *Diary of a Martian*, is to write a chapter and then immediately stop and read it. As I reread the chapter, I fix any issues that I find with form, grammar, spelling and so forth. I write fairly short chapters, so this process doesn't take long.

Once I have done this pass through the chapter, I paste the text into a tool like ProWritingAid and run the grammar and style reports. I fix any reported issues and then paste the text back into Scrivener.

While this does slow down the writing process a little, by performing a light edit, I am reasonably satisfied that the chapter is tidy, so I don't worry about it when I move on to the next chapter. I am not saying the chapter is finished and ready to release. I will always do another round of editing myself before sending it to a professional editor, but the text is fairly clean and presentable.

This process of cycling back through the chapters as I write them also means that when I finish a full first draft, the editing process is much easier to deal with than if I hadn't touched the draft at all, as the chapters are already in good condition. I often read about writers who practise the vomit draft technique, but then have a hell of a time when it comes to editing, as they have 80,000 or more messy words to work through; this, to me, is nowhere near as fun as the original writing process.

The idea of editing as you go can be controversial. Many writers argue that, in doing so, you are breaking your creative flow. But, for me, it has worked out well in preventing anxiety about the amount of editing required at the end of the project.

Thankfully, I had already settled into this writing process before I started *Diary of a Martian*. I wrote *The Art of Conversation*, *The Path to Freedom: Starting a Business for the Reluctant Entrepreneur* and *Powerful Presentations: Selling Your Story on Stage or in the Board-*

*room* using this process. By the time I started the novel, I already had my process set in stone, which meant I could focus on the story. I feel this really helped me write the book, because I was confident that I could get to the finish line.

## Getting into the Flow

One of the holy grails for any creative professional is to get into a flow state when working. A flow state means that you are so deeply focused on what you are doing that you have no sense of time. You start work and, before you know it, five hours has elapsed.

In the distracted world we live in, entering a flow state can feel like a challenge. All around us are machines that just want to beep and ping at us all day. It feels like our technology overlords are trying to prevent us from being creative in flow states.

I use music to help—particularly classical music or film scores. I can't listen to anything with lyrics as I find them distracting. Even though I like rock and metal music, which are all vocals, I just can't work with it playing. Don't get me started on modern pop songs; they don't make 'em like they used too. (Excuse me while I shake my fists and shout at the clouds.)

Baroque classical music works particularly well for me, though it's hard to explain why. Perhaps the slightly depressing minor key and slow tempo help calm me down and put my mind in the right state to be creative. It's not a style of music I have ever been a particular fan of before and certainly have never listened to for recreation. But I read that this style of music works well for students reviewing for exams, so I thought I would give it a go and was surprised by the results. It's like slipping into a trance and you just work.

As I write this very chapter, I am listening to someone go hell for leather on a harpsichord and I have been like this since nine in the morning, drafting chapters for this book. It doesn't feel like I have been writing for hours, but as I write this sentence, it is now 3:30 p.m.

Because this type of baroque classical music works so well, I reserve it for writing only. I never listen to it for pleasure or any reason other than writing. Luckily, most modern music streaming services contain hundreds of hours of classical recordings.

### Key Takeaways

Every writer eventually settles into their own writing process and it's impossible for any book to tell you what that process should be. If you are just starting off, then you will need to experiment to see what works for you. Perhaps you prefer the idea of the vomit draft, where you just write and don't look back until you finish the manuscript. If, like me, you find that idea stressful, you might attempt the light edit as you go and constantly cycle back to tidy up the chapters as you write them. Either way, it doesn't matter as long as you are comfortable with the process.

FOURTEEN

# Mental and Physical Health when Writing

As biological creatures, we are designed to move around and interact with people to stay healthy. As writers, we sit in a chair, hunched over a keyboard, in isolation from other living beings while we drive ourselves insane thinking about what to write and wracked with anxiety as we worry that the words we're writing are rubbish.

It's not the healthiest thing to be doing, and as someone on the wrong side of forty-five, I've had my fair share of complications from sitting behind a desk most of my professional life. Upper and lower back pain has been a feature of my working career and most of it stems from sitting behind the desk and not taking care of my posture.

Back pain became more of an issue during the COVID-19 lockdown. The setup I have at my rented business office is pretty good in terms of posture and ergonomics, but, when I had to work from home during lockdown, I established my office temporarily in my dining room. I do have a shared office at home with my wife, but we decided that both working in the same room was not a recipe for a happy marriage, so I set up downstairs. This meant I was sitting on a dining room chair, staring at a monitor that was not the correct height and using a keyboard that had no form of wrist support.

I should've known better because of my experience with back pain, but I did not expect the lockdown to last as long as it did. Once I realised I'd be working from home for a sustained period, I had to invest in some equipment to make myself comfortable. These investments included a monitor riser to elevate my monitor so I am not looking down, a better keyboard and wrist support to protect me from Repetitive Strain Injury (RSI) and a new office chair with lumbar support. A dining room chair feels more like a medieval torture device if you sit on it for more than two hours.

If you're reading this and are younger than I (under forty-five), then I urge you to take care of your posture when working from a desk, to protect your back and spine. The rest of this chapter will take you through a series of measures to protect not only your physical health, but also your mental well-being.

It's worth noting that I'm writing this all from my personal experience and not as a health expert. At first, I wasn't sure whether to include this chapter in a book about writing my first novel, but I decided that it's an important subject that few writers talk about, as all we really want to do is sit behind a desk and write without thinking of the consequences.

## Physical Health

While writing exercises your brain as you spill those words onto the computer via your keyboard, it has the potential to be terrible for your body. This means we need to start by talking about posture and ergonomics. If, like me, you have worked in an office environment for most of your career, you will no doubt have sat through some mandatory corporate training on desk ergonomics. Companies put you through these training sessions so that you remain healthy and don't take off sick time because of a bad back, neck or wrists.

Like me, you probably rolled your eyes at such courses and skipped through them as fast as you could because they are boring. Well, let me take on the role of that annoying health and safety officer with their clipboard—apologies if you are a health and safety officer with a clipboard in real life.

How you sit at your desk and write is so important that, if you get it wrong, you could limit the amount of writing you are capable of and, therefore, the number of books you can write in your life. Bet that got your attention.

What you want to avoid is bending your back and neck. You need to keep your back straight and, to do this, you need a chair with a high back and lumbar support that presses into the base of your back, as you can see in the following illustration. Your eyes need to be level with the top of the monitor, so that you can glance down at the screen without bending your neck or spine.

Many monitor models on the market come with height-adjustable stands, so it will be easy to adjust the monitor. I use a monitor that doesn't allow you to adjust the height, so I use a small shelf on the desk to raise the computer by about five inches from the desk, putting the top of the screen in line with my eyes.

## On Writing Your First Novel

Picture from Adobe Stock

If you look at the diagram on the left, you see that the person in the seat has their feet raised. Raising your feet will straighten your legs and help you keep your back straight. With your feet raised, slouching and bending your spine feels strange and unnatural, forcing you to fix your posture.

Last, you need to note what you do with your wrists on the desk. If you use a large keyboard and the front is raised from the desk, it is advisable to use a wrist support in front of the keyboard. Without a wrist support, your hands and wrist will be bent and you risk getting a strain in your wrist and lower arm. There are many wrist supports on the market, from memory foam to blocks of plastic or wood. You don't need to spend much, but they will make a vast difference in your comfort level. I use an Apple Magic keyboard, which is very flat and shallow on the desk, so I don't need a wrist support for this keyboard. For any other keyboard, however, I use a foam support. If you make these simple adjustments to your desk setup, you will do your body a massive favour.

A high-quality chair is also quite important. Most reasonably priced office chairs offer decent back support, so you don't need to spend much. When I set up my temporary office at home in the dining room, I looked on eBay and found a reconditioned Herman Miller Aeron chair for a fraction of its original and eye-watering price. Even though it is second-hand and looks a little worn, it's one of the most comfortable chairs I've ever used.

One particular invention has been an absolute blessing for writers, or any desk-based professional, and that is the standing desk. Standing desks come in many forms, from electric sit/stand desks you can raise and lower with buttons to hand-winched desks to mechanical risers that you place on a conventional desk. The type of desk isn't important, but the benefit you receive is staggering, as you can move from an unhealthy sitting position to standing, and vice versa.

Back in 2018, I invested in an electric sit/stand desk, and it's built like a tank. I expect the desk will outlast me. Every day that I am in the office, I move from sitting to standing several times throughout the day. When I arrive at the office and go through emails, business accounts and other administrative tasks, I put the desk in standing mode. When I write or perform any other creative work, I start off sitting and, every hour, I go back to standing for half an hour.

Since using this desk, I have noticed that I have more energy throughout the day. I am not faced with the afternoon fatigue slump, because I am more active, which means I can complete more writing or other creative work during the day. I have also stabilised my weight—and even lost some—just by standing more. When I first used the standing desk, I could feel some aching in my muscles, but that was a good thing, as it meant I was using muscle groups during the day that I hadn't used as much before. To make using a standing desk more comfortable, you can buy a rubber/silicon anti-fatigue mat for the floor. By standing on this mat and not on a hard floor, you reduce the level of tiredness in your feet.

You don't have to spend a fortune on one of these desks. Desk risers that let you lift your computer, monitor and keyboard to a satisfactory level are quite affordable and the benefits for your posture, activity levels and energy throughout the day are huge.

## Mental Health

Looking after your physical health is very important if you want to last as a writer and not be plagued with a bad back or neck, but looking after your mental health is just as important. Writing is a solitary affair. To write a book, you need your bottom in a chair and you have to write furiously.

This level of isolation can be seen as either a benefit or a drawback, depending on your personality. I am an introvert, so I love spending time by myself in isolation. I use solitude to recharge my mental batteries. That doesn't mean I am shy. As part of my 'day job', I am a public speaker. I travel to conferences all over the world to deliver talks in packed auditoriums and I love it. But when I get offstage, I have already planned out my exit route back to the hotel so I can recharge. It suits me just fine.

For extroverts, sitting by yourself all day to write may be very hard, as you require social interactions to fuel your mental energy. I think it's extroverts who may struggle the most with the solitude of writing. Still, even as an introvert, I need human contact and I enjoy talking to like-minded professionals.

I don't enjoy working from home, so I rent an office that I work from for most of the working week. I love working from my rented office, but I'm there by myself and it can get a little lonely if I do that every day, so I also use a local co-working space once a week. Why? Because there are other workers there who are running their own small businesses and it's nice to go in and work around other people for a day. Everyone is busy, but you still get office banter, just like when I worked at other companies. Because everyone in the co-working office is a freelancer, you don't have to put up with any office politics. Using the co-working space for half a day or a day at a time isn't expensive and I gain fulfilling social interactions that bring important mental health benefits.

So, the first tip is, if you are writing alone, make sure you interact with other people. If you already work a full-time office job and write for fun in the evenings, social interaction may not be such a big problem, but, if you ever become a full-time writer, these interactions are an important health consideration.

I miss little about my past corporate life, but I do miss some people I worked with. We are social creatures. No matter how introverted you think you are, as humans, we all require a minimum level of social interaction. Thanks to spending a day a week in a co-working space, I have met a range of interesting people, including an illustrator and graphic designer who may end up designing some book covers for me. Talking to people is good for business, too.

Taking regular breaks is another important aspect of mental health, particularly when you spend a lot of time writing and are in the zone, getting those words down on the page. Earlier in the book, I talked about writing sprints where you write for twenty minutes and then take a quick break away from your screen. Writing sprints are a fantastic technique for forcing breaks into your writing time. In addition to taking these shorter breaks, it is a good idea to get outside for a short walk. Even if you are not writing during the day and work a regular job, going outside will help you, even if it's only for a quick stroll around the block.

There are many benefits to walking. First, you get some exercise, which is never a bad thing. You also breathe in some fresh air—unless you live in a smog-filled city. I feel very fortunate to live in a small town in Derbyshire in the United Kingdom, where I am surrounded by hills, trees and open skies. I can walk two minutes from the office and be in the countryside, where you wouldn't even realise there was a small town nearby. I try to tell my kids how lucky they are to live so close to all this greenery, but they just shrug, barely looking up from their phones. They'll get it one day.

Getting in plenty of steps is something I am quite fanatical about. In the morning, I walk my son to school instead of driving. That's a twenty-minute walk. Then, I walk to the office, which takes another fifteen minutes. Then, in the afternoon, I have to walk back to the school to pick up my son. These enforced walking breaks make all the difference, as they drag me away from the screen.

I like to track all this walking using an Apple Watch, although any fitness tracker, such as a Fitbit or a Garmin, does the same thing. I have set quite a high daily goal on the Apple Watch, and I ensure that I close each of those exercise rings each day, which means I have to achieve a specific calorie burn and number of minutes of exercise with an elevated heart rate. I also have to maintain ten hours a day of standing for at least ten minutes in an hour. This is easy to do with a standing desk in the office. Using a fitness tracker, no matter the model, turns simple daily exercise into a game.

By focusing on daily walking, I feel I have more energy, am fitter and remain in a good mood most of the time. Before focusing on this exercise routine, I would often feel down or deflated with work, but that has all changed now that I get a decent level of exercise.

I have never been a gym fanatic. I joined a gym once but hated it, so daily walking is my alternative. I may not run a 5k race or marathon, but my general fitness levels are pretty good and I achieved this by making minor adjustments in my working day.

Walking and daily exercise aren't just about physical fitness. They are just as, if not more, important for mental fitness. Runners often talk about a 'runner's high'—the sensation of elation after going for a run. You can feel just as good going for a walk outside in fresh air. You don't have to run or jog, if that's not for you. A brisk walk that gets your heart pumping can feel great and it costs nothing.

## Key Takeaways

While this isn't a book about fitness and mental health, they are two subjects that any writer should take seriously. Writing is a solitary affair that can see you hunched over your keyboard. If you don't take corrective action to improve your posture and look after your mental health, you will affect your ability to write books long into the future. A few minor adjustments now could help you continue to write books long into old age.

FIFTEEN

# Positive Mental Attitude

I wanted to talk a little about a positive mental attitude with your writing. Though related to the previous chapter on health, I feel this subject is so important that it warrants its own chapter. If you think about your whole body, it is just a big bag of blood, guts, bones and muscle with this grey squishy thing on top—biology wasn't my strongest subject at school.

That grey, squishy thing inside your head, otherwise known as your brain, is an amazing part of your body. It's responsible for all your thoughts throughout the day. Your brain is also your biggest saboteur, and if you're not careful, it will do its best to ruin everything.

When I talked about mental and physical health when writing, I suggested a few techniques to aid in your general mental health. However, there is more to mental health than just getting a good night of sleep. How you think, both in your conscious and subconscious mind, can impact your ability to write and complete a large, complex project such as writing a novel. Subtle shifts in your thought process and outlook on life can make all the difference.

One way of shaping your thought processes in ways that benefit your writing is through the law of attraction, which is a spiritual way of looking at how we frame activities in our lives. When I say spiritual, I don't mean airy fairy. In this chapter, I will not encourage you to sit cross-legged on the floor and start humming or anything like that, though certainly feel free to do that if you enjoy it. But it's possible to train your mind in a way that ensures good things happen in your life as opposed to all the horrible problems that life can throw at you.

## Law of Attraction

I was practising the law of attraction long before I knew what it was called or what it was about and I believe it has helped me succeed in my career and life over the years. The law of attraction is about projecting positive thoughts/energy out into the universe that attract positive energy back to you. Sounds weird, I know, but stick with it, as it's not as strange as it sounds.

Another explanation is that the law of attraction is the ability to attract into our lives whatever we are focusing on. This is a little like confirmation bias, where you seek information that confirms what you already believe. Well, if you believe that you are a successful writer, what's going to happen? You'll seek out what you need to make that a reality. There is a brilliant book, now made into a TV documentary, called *The Secret*, by Rhonda Byrne that I recommend reading or watching, as it goes into much greater detail than I can in this book. Basically, it shows how you can achieve anything you want in life if you put your mind in a positive state.

Let's consider a non-writing example that I think most people can relate to. Imagine you are in financial debt. This could be due to an overbearing mortgage, credit cards, loans and so forth. Being in debt isn't a pleasant experience, especially if the repayments run away from you. The law of attraction holds that if you constantly think about debt and struggle to make the payments, all you will ever know is debt. You won't escape it. The more you think about being in debt, the worse it will get. Your constant thoughts about debt are negative energy that you are projecting into the world, and it will seem that all you get back is debt—mounting interest payments, paying debt with debt and other continual struggles.

You may try to be positive by thinking or saying to yourself:

'I am going to get out of debt'.
'I am going to focus on one debt first and pay it off'.

But you are still thinking about debt, even if you are trying to put a positive spin on those thoughts. And guess what happens? The same problems persist. So, what does the law of attraction say you should do, instead? Well, you still need to think positive thoughts, but you need to reframe them to something like:

'I am going to seek a pay raise at work'.
'I am going to double my income by taking on some freelancing work'.
'I am going to change my job to a better-paying company'.
'I am going to be in a position where money comes to me'.

These positive thoughts are not about the debt. You are not using that word. Instead, you are framing your position differently. You need to condition your mind to have thoughts like these examples. Of course, this isn't magic. You don't just have positive thoughts, and suddenly everything goes well. There isn't a magic money tree that will send money your way, but by putting out these positive thoughts, you will be more likely to act on them. Your mind will know that if these thoughts come true, you will have a better job, more money and a way to pay down those debts. Your new, positive outlook will give you a bias for action.

Your brain is a muscle and, like the rest of your body, it needs exercising. Reframing your thoughts is something you need to practice many times a day, every day for weeks, months and years. You are trying to reprogram your subconscious. When you do this, your brain will subtly influence the rest of your body and you will start acting on your dreams.

I have lived my life like this for many years. I have always been positive about family life and my career and always knew what I wanted from life, especially when building a career after university. There are three categories of thought process you can work with to help: affirmations, visualisation and gratitude. Let's examine them individually and then I will show how I apply these to writing in general and the writing of *Diary of a Martian*, which is, of course, why you are here.

**Affirmations**. Affirmations are positive statements that help you reframe your thoughts to stop self-sabotage and negativity. They are a great way to increase your self-confidence and belief in your own abilities. An affirmation is a statement that you read to yourself, either in thought or out loud. By repeating affirmations, you can reprogram your mind. Some examples of affirmations might be:

'I am a confident person'.

'I am successful'.
'All I need is within me right now'.
'I am motivated to conquer the day'.
'I am a successful writer'.
'I am a successful software developer'.
'I am a good husband'.
'I am a good father'.

Your affirmations can remain at a high level, as in these examples, or they can be more specific. The important point is they are all positive and should motivate you. When you have a list of affirmations that are specific to you, read them to yourself several times a day: when you wake up, during the day and before you go to bed. Nobody needs to know you are doing it. They are personal to you, but, over time, your attitude and outlook on life will shift.

**Visualisation**. Visualisation is about taking your goals and dreams and imagining what success looks and feels like. It's a great excuse to spend some time daydreaming. Let's imagine, for example, that you really want to run a 5k race or a half-marathon—or even a full marathon for the really fit among you. Any of those options is a huge undertaking if you don't run regularly. I'm reasonably fit, but I would struggle to run a 5k race. This means I would need to train and prepare for the race. That amount of work can appear daunting.

With visualisation, you imagine yourself running the race. As you are running, imagine how you feel: you feel great, you are making good progress, it's a nice sunny day, you feel amazing, you can feel the burn in your muscles as you run, but you are taking in lungfuls of fresh air. Then imagine yourself crossing the finish line. The crowds lining the tracks are cheering. You stop, take a large drink of water and receive your medal for completing the race. Visualise how proud you feel of this achievement. Imagine the faces and reactions of your family who are at the finishing line.

By visualising yourself completing the race, you're more likely to take the steps to make that visualisation a reality, as your mind has already had a taste of what success feels like. It's a powerful technique that works if you visualise that success often. It was remarkably effective for the writing of my novel, as I will explain in a moment.

**Gratitude**. It's important in life to be thankful and give gratitude for everything nice that happens to you. In the United States, they even dedicate Thanksgiving Day to it in November. Giving gratitude isn't complicated and you can give thanks either verbally or silently if you don't want anyone to hear.

Being actively grateful has many benefits. First, it makes us happier. Just think how it feels when someone does something nice for you. You thank them, which makes them smile. Then you feel great. Being grateful also helps reduce stress, build self-esteem and improve personal relationships, as other people feel valued.

All you need to do is say or think what you are grateful for, though if you are giving thanks to someone else, saying it out loud to them is important. Using the running analogy mentioned above, you might say:

> 'I'm grateful to run today'.
> 'I'm grateful to be fit and healthy'.
> 'I'm grateful that the weather is nice for running today'.
> 'I'm grateful that my family supports my running goals'.

Try it several times a day: when you wake up, at midday and before you go to bed. Just run through what you are grateful for. Turn it into a habit, along with reading your affirmations and visualisations. Over time, they help shift your outlook on life.

## Application to Writing

I know what you're thinking: 'That's great, Steve, but this is a book about writing'. True, so let's talk about writing. I have applied these techniques throughout my career—first, in software development and leadership, then, in my business of creating online training content and writing nonfiction books and now with writing my first novel. Let's go through my approach to affirmations, visualisation and gratitude. You will see just how easy this is to do. (The trick is constant repetition.)

**Affirmations**. So many times, I've seen someone with the dream to write a book. They create a new word processor file and begin typing Chapter One. But when they speak about their writing, they say something like, 'I really want to be a writer' or 'One day, I will be a successful writer'.

The problem with this is they are already setting themselves up for potential failure, as their language isn't conducive to success. And I get it; it's a self-confidence issue. If you are just starting out with writing, but you say you are a writer, it puts a level of expectation on you and your work. Still, I believe you need to be affirmative with your language. When I first wrote a nonfiction book, I immediately acted like a writer by repeating statements to myself, such as:

'I am a writer'.

'I am writing a fantastic book that people will want to read'.
'I am worthy of being a writer'.
'I deserve to be a writer'.
'My words have meaning'.

Even though I was just starting out writing a book at the time, I thought like a writer. And why shouldn't I have? I have done the same with *Diary of a Martian*. Even from the very beginning, with that first germ of an idea during the January 2021 COVID-19 lockdown in the United Kingdom, I knew I was a writer of children's fiction.

You may think that words like these make you seem very sure of yourself, and yeah, I guess they do. But the affirmations you repeat are designed for you and nobody else. I didn't run through the streets shouting that I'm a children's fiction writer. That would be a strange thing to do. Yet, in the little world within my mind, I was a writer. And a damned good one. The only other person who knew these affirmations was my wife and she has similar views on positive thinking to me.

So, what are some affirmations I used for *Diary of a Martian*? Glad you asked.

'I am a successful children's novelist'.
'I have written and published a science fiction series for younger readers'.
'Children love my books, adventures and characters'.
'I am full of creative ideas'.
'I am pursuing my goal of writing an amazing novel'.
'My story is important'.
'My story is entertaining'.

These are a few of the affirmations that I use and I repeat

them to myself every day. Did they work? Did I finish the novel? Well, if you are reading this book, then yes, as I'm publishing it at the same time as *Diary of a Martian*. It wouldn't make sense to publish this book without the actual novel in question being available.


**Visualisations**. I am a very visual person, and I am very grateful for this (more on that in a moment). On daydreaming, I consider myself an expert. I could sit there for hours staring out the window, lost in another world. To me, daydreaming is productive, as that's where many of my ideas come from—long showers and walks. As an aside, being a daydreamer was often incompatible with my earlier career. I recall the number of times my manager had a 'word' with me for just looking out the window, even though I was just trying to think through a complex problem and its solution. I don't think he was a visual thinker. He just didn't get it. Even with creative writing, those times just staring into space and thinking—that's writing. It's all part of the process.

Visualisations have played a major part in writing *Diary of a Martian* and have helped propel me towards the finish line. Because writing a novel is such a large project, I like to visualise success the same way you would plan milestones on a large corporate project. I have visualised various stages throughout the novel's production and publication. I visualise four stages regularly.


*Stage 1: Completing the first draft*. The first visualisation is of completing the first draft. How would you feel if you completed your manuscript? You would feel pretty damned good, that's for sure. If your book was, for example, 80,000 words, that's a lot of words and pages. Writing that much is a feat that you should be proud of. I try to imagine what it's like to write 'The End', then sit back and admire my work, seeing all those chapters lined up there in Scrivener.

**Stage 2: Receiving the first print proof.** The next visualisation is receiving the first print proof of the book, which applies to indie publishing as much as it does to traditional publishing, as you will always receive a print proof of your book to check. I already know how great it feels when the mail-person delivers that package, so I try to recapture that moment in my mind. Gently opening the cardboard envelope and sliding the book out of the box, ready for a first glimpse of your hard work as a physical product. Even a subtle sniff of the pages. There's nothing like the smell of a book fresh off the press.

**Stage 3: Publication day**. My next visualisation is publication day. You can imagine how exciting it is when your hard work pays off, and the book is available to the public. You load up Amazon and you see that the book is available. You scroll down, and there's a sales rank. That means someone has bought it. As you check throughout the day, the sales rank number becomes lower and lower. Then you see someone has left a review—five stars! You've made it. You're not only a writer but a published author. It's a great feeling and visualising it helps motivate me to continue writing.

**Stage 4: Releasing more books in the series**. My final visualisation is grand. I planned for *Diary of a Martian* to be a trilogy, but there will be scope to write more if the demand is there, which is where this visualisation comes in. I imagine the series has taken off, big time. Taken off in Harry Potter style. A guy's gotta dream big. In this visualisation, I imagine that I am about to release book five. I have a public relations company working with me, and they have organised a large ticketed event. The event starts at 6 p.m. They filled the hall with my target audience—in this case, nine-to-twelve-year-old children and their parents.

The lights dim, the music plays. We have a smoke machine for dramatic effect. I take a seat on stage and look out at the children sitting there, wanting to hear a reading from the next book. A lot of the children are in costume as various characters from the previous books. The thought of children loving the characters so much that they want to dress up as them is quite heart-warming.

Okay, I admit, this one is a little out there. But I need some motivation for writing the rest of the series and I like the feeling of this visualisation. It may appear that I am being overconfident, but this is a technique to keep me motivated. Nobody knows I am visualising this, as I keep it to my imagination—well, you now know, but you'll keep it a secret. Right?

**Gratitude**. To me, being grateful is very important. It doesn't take long to be grateful, and it costs nothing. There are so many life events and problems that could hinder you from living your life and realising your dreams, but it's important to be mindful of everything that goes well in your life. From a writing point of view, I'm grateful for many things and I remind myself of these every day.

First, I am grateful for good health. To write a book, it helps if you are feeling well. I am grateful for not only physical health but also mental health, which I attribute largely to trying to remain positive, as discussed in this chapter. Without good health, writing would be much harder.

Next, I am grateful for being a visual thinker. I've always had an active imagination, and I'm grateful for it. The mind produces imagery that is much richer than anything on TV. Did you know that some people can't visualise stories or objects? It's a condition called aphantasia, which the Oxford English dictionary defines as 'the inability to form mental images of objects that are not present'. I am grateful I don't have to surmount that.

I am also grateful for having an active imagination. My list of story ideas will keep me writing well into old age. Once I have written one novel and proved to myself that it can be done (and if you are reading this book, I have proven it can be, as this book is being released at the same time as my novel), I can only go forwards.

I am also grateful for a supportive family. My wife has always encouraged my ideas and creative endeavours. My children are also interested and talk with me about my story ideas. They are also the first people outside those involved in the production process to read the novel and provide feedback and they are tough critics to impress.

These are just a few examples of my writing-based gratitude. There are many more facets, but you get the idea.

## Key Takeaways

The human mind is a powerful tool. It is capable of greatness but also of self-sabotage. I encourage you to think about what you are grateful for and to do this daily. This, combined with daily visualisation (or day dreaming, if you want to call it that) and affirmations, are powerful techniques to gradually reprogram your thoughts and general outlook on life.

It's not magic, though. By using this approach, you will not magically write a novel. You still need your bottom in a chair—or feet at a standing desk—and your hands on the keyboard (or with a pen or microphone). However, shifting your outlook on life and work can give you the motivation and staying power to see your dreams through. It really works if you put in the effort.

SIXTEEN

## The Danger of Comparison

It is said that as a writer, you should also be an avid reader. Not everyone agrees with that sentiment, but I do. The more you write, the more you analyse every book you read through a writer's eye. That can be a little annoying when you just want to enjoy a novel, but monitoring how another writer has structured and developed their story is a valuable and healthy skill. But beware; valuable analysis of another writer's style and craft can soon turn into a toxic habit where you constantly compare your abilities to those of other writers.

We all do it. I am no different. At the beginning of this book, I talked about why it took me so long to start creative writing. I was in my forties before I started writing stories seriously, even though it was always something I had long dreamed of doing. I regret all those wasted years.

I hesitated because I couldn't see how I could write to the same standard as a novel I picked up at the bookshop—a completed novel that has gone through multiple rounds of professional developmental, copy and line editing and proofreading. Of course, my early attempts couldn't compare.

I have since overcome that issue, but I have encountered another comparison problem. I aimed *Diary of a Martian* at a middle-grade audience of nine- to twelve-year-olds. While I was planning my story, I tried to read as many middle-grade books as I could from authors like J. K. Rowling, Eoin Colfer, etc. I enjoy them. It's a fun age group to write for and to read, even as an adult.

When I began my first draft of *Diary of a Martian*, I was working my way through the Artemis Fowl series. Then, something interesting happened. While I was in middle-grade writing mode, I became nearly obsessed with thinking about what I was reading and comparing it to what I was writing. Comparing my writing to that of Eoin Colfer, a very experienced novelist, was not the best idea for my motivation.

Because I was in middle-grade writing mode, my brain found it difficult to switch off from that genre. As I read one of the Artemis Fowl books, I constantly compared everything. Sentence length, paragraph length. Does he have a prologue? Does he use many adverbs? First or third person? How many point-of-view characters does he have? And so on and so on.

In the end, I had to stop reading because I wasn't enjoying the book. The book itself was excellent, but I just couldn't enjoy it while comparing every single facet of Colfer's writing to mine.

I picked up another novel, this time a thriller by A. G. Riddle. Because it's not a middle-grade book, I didn't compare Riddle's writing to my own. Why? Because it was a different genre and aimed at a different audience, so mentally, I didn't feel the need to make the comparison. The brain is a funny old contraption.

To show just how weird the brain is, while writing this very book, I have been reading a few writing craft books, but I haven't felt the need to compare this book to them. I have no idea why. I just didn't feel the need. But while writing *Diary of a Martian*, I haven't been able to touch another middle-grade book.

My solution to this problem was easy. Until my novel is written, I will just avoid other middle-grade books. That means when I finish writing *Diary of a Martian*, I will most likely have to binge read some novels before I start work on the sequel, but I'm okay with that. It gives me something to look forward to.

When I thought through the comparison problem in more detail, I realised how silly it is. Here I was comparing myself to Eoin Colfer. His multiple-book Artemis Fowl series has sold millions by a major traditional publisher and has even been adapted into a movie by Disney. It really is a daft comparison to make. If I want to compare myself to anyone, I should pick a debut author who is just ahead of me with their first book.

An aspiring novelist comparing their writing ability to a seasoned professional with a vast audience makes no sense if that comparison is going to stop your ability to write. You are much better off not reading those books—my chosen approach—and just getting the book written. At least once you have a completed novel, you then have something to use for comparison. But even then, a first draft work-in-progress can't be compared to an edited and published novel.

Once my novel has been written, edited and proofread, I will then need to consider comparisons, but not to analyse my writing style in relation to another writer. Part of the publishing process is to find comparable books on the market. That requires you to look in the same genre categories as your book to see what similar books are there, particularly books that are selling well. This process is important, as, at that point, you are looking for inspiration for cover designs and book blurbs; so, at that stage, comparison is fine—but not when you are still drafting.

## Key Takeaways

Comparing your writing to that of other writers while you are trying to draft can have a detrimental effect on your own writing and motivation. If you compare your work-in-progress to, say, Stephen King, you are always going to be at a disadvantage. He has written so many novels and had so much success that it isn't even a fair fight.

I strongly recommend not reading books in your work-in-progress genre while you are drafting if it will impede your writing process. Don't stop reading books, but maybe use your drafting period as an opportunity to read books you might not ordinarily read.

SEVENTEEN

# Getting to the First Draft Finish Line

Once I passed my initial thirty percent honeymoon slump and crisis of confidence, I could pick up the pace and motor through the second act of the story. The planned beats from my beat sheet didn't change; I just had to get the words down, which I did over the space of three months. My pace also picked up once I'd completed the Faber Academy novel writing course, as I no longer had any coursework commitments. My writing pace varied from day to day. If my day job was busy, I would try to maintain a minimum writing habit of three short bursts of 350 words, which ensured that I kept forward momentum.

Once I had written and reviewed three to five chapters, I would tidy them up and send them in batches to my critique partner for comments. As that feedback came in, I would implement anything that was a quick fix immediately. Anything bigger that required structural changes, I would note in a document for the later revision stages.

As the book developed, I put a timetable and a series of deadlines in place so I had dates to work towards. My plan was to complete the first draft by the end of July, when the schools close for the summer holidays. Then, I would take the six weeks of holiday away from the book and pick up the revisions when the schools restarted. As June began, I was coming to the end of writing the second act and preparing for the big finale. I estimated that I had about six chapters to write before the major final sequence.

Towards the end of June, the Glastonbury Festival, a huge music and arts event, was happening in Somerset, United Kingdom. I didn't have tickets, but the BBC was covering the festival on TV all weekend. My wife had already arranged a weekend away with some friends, and my son and daughter were also staying at friends' houses, meaning I had a rare weekend all to myself. I intended to make good use of this time, so, with the Glastonbury festival coverage for company, I made myself comfortable to write as much as I could.

As far as writing weekends go, it was perfect. I got into a state of productive flow and the words spilled out. I realised that I could reach the end of the first draft that weekend if I put the hours in. That thought alone was a huge motivation for me to get the book finished. The light at the end of the tunnel was now burning bright.

On Saturday, I worked in longer one-hour sprints with breaks in between. Once in the morning and once in the afternoon, I would go out for a walk to make sure I wasn't sitting all weekend. I ended up writing until 3 a.m., which is very late for me. I'm not good at late nights.

After waking late on Sunday, I read through my work from the day before and made a few minor changes, mostly fixing typos and some clunky sentences. Then, with six or seven chapters left until the end, I settled down to finish the book. I'd already completed the final action sequence, so I was left with some winding down scenes and wrapping up loose ends.

By 6 p.m. on Sunday—just before my wife and kids walked in the door—I completed my first draft of *Diary of a Martian*. I was elated. The long road from the initial idea to that point had taken me through the Faber Academy course and the ups and downs of putting words on the page. I allowed myself a few days to bask in the glory of completing a first draft, but I knew I still had a lot of work to do.

My initial goal had been to complete the first draft by the end of July, but because I had finished a month before, I started some of the editing process early. I planned to tackle editing in two stages. The first was to address my initial snag list of minor changes and the second was to take on the larger issues of structure and character voice. The snag list I could fix before the summer holidays, and the larger edits could wait until after the holidays, once I had some mental distance from the manuscript. I cover these stages in more detail in the next chapter.

## Key Takeaways

As I've discussed earlier in this book, working past the first thirty percent in a writing project can be tough, as all you see is a huge mountain of work ahead of you. Eventually, however, you make enough progress in the project that you see a little glimmer of light at the end of that literary tunnel. When you see that light, there is nothing for it but to hunker down and get the words on the page.

I found the race to the end quite motivating; the closer I came to the end of the draft the more motivated I became. In this first-draft stage, you don't need to worry about writing the highest-quality prose. You just want to get the story down. If I'm honest with myself, those last six or so chapters that I was knocking out before my kids ran through the door were not my finest writing examples. I was certainly rushing to reach the end, and those final chapters required a fair amount of editing and revision to knock them into shape, but that's fine. The story was there. It just needed some work.

The sense of achievement I felt at the end of the first draft was immense. I had written a full novel. My final manuscript was just over 78,000 words. I knew it was too long and that I'd have to make some cuts, but I preferred a book that was too long for my target readership than too short.

With the first draft complete, I now had the huge—and important—job of editing and revising.

EIGHTEEN

# Climbing the Self-Editing Mountain

As I was working on the first draft of *Diary of a Martian*, I was also working on this book to make sure I was capturing my true thoughts and feelings as I created the story for my first novel. Once I completed the first draft, I deliberately put this book on pause for a while. I didn't want to write about the editing process until I had completed it, which is what I have done.

Sitting beside me as I write this chapter is a stack of copies of *Diary of a Martian* in their final form, ready for to be sold. I can't describe how exciting it is to be able to pick up and flip through my completed novel. The sense of accomplishment is huge, and I have worked hard to produce a book that looks as good as any you would find in a bookshop.

Pausing the current book until I had finished editing *Diary of a Martian* was important, as editing is a huge part of the writing process. I had been through the editing process on many books before *Diary of a Martian* with both traditional publishers and through self-publishing routes, so I already had insight into what works and what doesn't.

In this chapter, I am going to walk through how I approached my self-editing process for the novel, and in the next chapter, I talk about what it's like to work with professional editors. I have collaborated with many editors throughout my career. Most have been excellent, some not so good. My aim is to help you decide how to pick an editor to work with.

## What Doesn't Work for Me

When I wrote my first book—a non-fiction book about the agile software development process (it's as dull as it sounds)—I embarked on the self-editing process once I hit the first draft stage. My approach was to start on page one and work my way through the book.

For me, this was a terrible slog. It was very cumbersome to wade through the book, start to finish, line by line, and attempt to analyse everything I had written. Perhaps from a copy-editing standpoint, this approach is necessary, but the initial editing stages are not about individual line edits. They are more about looking at the structure and message of the book. Are the characters realistic? Are you making use of all five senses in your descriptions, etc.? Spelling, grammar and so forth should come later. Working through a book line by line is also just very boring and by the time you reach the end, you may not be giving the text your full attention.

When I worked on another non-fiction book of mine, *The Path to Freedom: Starting a Business for the Reluctant Entrepreneur*, I took a different approach to my early editing, as that book was 150,000 words. As I wrote each chapter and worked my way through the first draft, I would take notes on what I needed to change or any issues I thought were in the book. I held off from fixing all these issues up front because I wanted to focus on completing the first draft. When the draft was finished, I made the fixes, then reread the book and made further notes. I did this several times until I had a book that I thought was of high quality and ready to go to a professional editor.

This way of working, which I found more fun and less tedious than working through the book line by line, drove my approach for *Diary of a Martian*. As an ex-corporate guy who likes documentation and diagrams, I have distilled the editing process I used into a flowchart, which you can see in the following diagram. As I mentioned, I completed the editing process before writing this chapter to ensure that I could write about the process in its entirety, knowing if it worked for me or not.

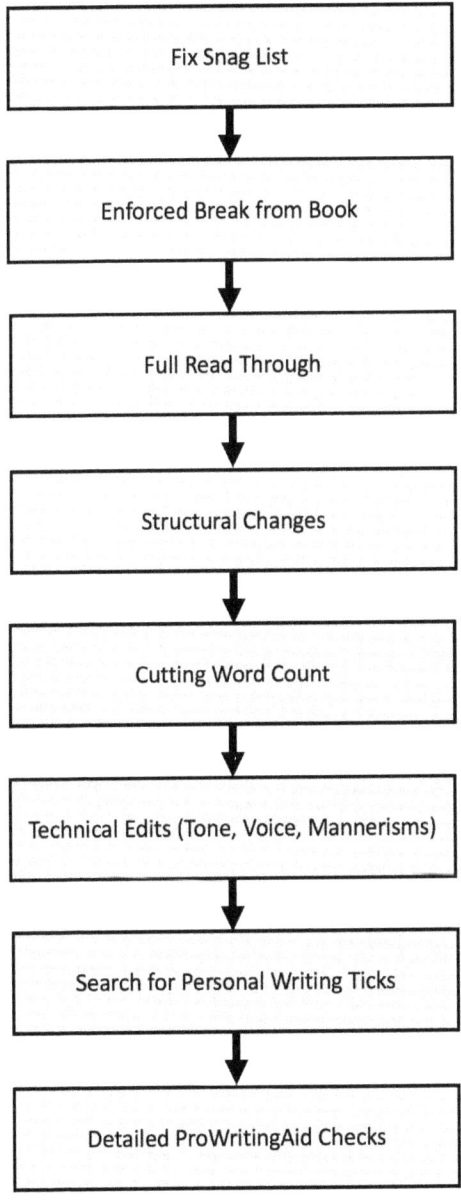

Self-Editing Workflow

You may feel that this process looks a bit too formal or rigid, but I don't believe it is. Diagrams make everything look formal, but I believe having a plan helps you to be more efficient during the editing phase. When I started editing *Diary of a Martian*, I drew that diagram on my whiteboard and stuck with it. I went through each of those steps and, at the end, I was ready to send the book out for a professional edit. That doesn't mean each stage was easy. Editing a book is hard—just as hard as drafting —but breaking the process down into smaller pieces helped me work through the complexity. I will discuss each of the steps in the diagram later in this chapter.

## Editing for Pantsers vs. Plotters

The editing experience can feel very different for a writer, depending on whether you are a pantser or an outliner. I covered pantsing and outlining earlier in the book, but from an editing perspective, if you're a pantser and make up the story as you go along, the editing process may be quite tough, as you likely have a more unstructured story to knock into shape. In other words, you might have put off thinking about structure until the end.

With outlining, you front-load the planning and structuring of your story, so when you reach the editing phase, the resulting first draft will have a clearer structure, which may make the editing process more straightforward. Of course, there will always be exceptions, depending on a writer's skill level and experience, but from talking to many writers, I've heard that people who write a story by the seat of their pants can find the initial editing period stressful.

I consider myself a plantser: someone who sits between plotting and pantsing. I went into writing my novel with a well-developed beat sheet that was detailed enough to guide my writing and give me the novel's structure, but also loose enough that I could practice some discovery writing and make up scenes.

Because of my pre-planning, when I reached the editing stage, the number of necessary large and sweeping structural changes was minimal and those changes I had to implement were straightforward.

So, let's run through the steps in my editing flow chart and I'll talk through the changes I had to make to my first draft. Your editing experience will be different, depending on the type of book you are writing, but I hope this serves as a good example.

## Fix Snag List

As I wrote my first draft, I kept a separate document called 'my snag list'. On it, I noted all the changes I wanted to make that would take me longer than half an hour to fix—that is, changes that would slow me down too much if I made them immediately. Because I finished my first draft a month ahead of my schedule, I decided to try to work through as much of the snag list as possible before taking a break from the book over the summer holidays.

The first snag I wanted to tackle was chapter length. *Diary of a Martian* is a middle-grade reader aimed at nine- to twelve-year-olds, but quite a few of my chapters felt long at 3,000–4,000 words. But dividing the chapters wasn't easy. Because the book is a 'diary', each chapter starts with a date representing when the events in that chapter happened. How was I going to deal with long chapters that were set on a particular day?

I tried to keep chapters down to 1,500 words or fewer, unless I couldn't find a good split point. All the chapters, apart from two, ended up obeying the rules. When I split a chapter (leaving me with several chapters happening on the same day), I decided to omit the date at the start of the chapter; so, if a date is missing, it means the events take place on the same date as the previous chapter.

Once I had completed the chapter splits, my book grew from twenty-nine chapters to fifty-four, but each chapter was a much quicker read. This had been a goal of mine—to create short and digestible chapters that a child could complete easily in an evening reading session. In the middle-grade reading range, you need to factor in a wider scope of reading abilities, from the reluctant reader to the child who reads beyond their age. With shorter chapters, you enable a less-able reader to gain a sense of achievement by finishing a chapter, while more experienced readers can propel themselves through multiple chapters with ease.

Another change I made was around speech marks. I wrote *Diary of a Martian* in British English, as this is my native form of the language; this meant I used the single speech mark in my first draft, as is standard in British English. Because I am publishing the book myself, I only want to deal with one manuscript for all English-speaking territories, rather than British, US and other versions. In summer 2022, I attended a self-publishing conference and, during lunch, I engaged in an interesting conversation with other, more experienced fiction authors and publishers, many of whom also wrote in British English. They believed that US readers were quite tolerant of British English, but several pointed out that, in some reviews, they had been criticised by US readers for using single speech marks instead of double speech marks.

The advice of these authors, many of whom were selling large numbers of books in a series, was that British English is fine, but single speech marks can be a step too far. Taking heed of their advice, I changed my manuscript. Scrivener has a tool that lets you highlight only speech in the manuscript, so making this change only took an afternoon.

Another change I wanted to make in the early stage of edits was to gender swap one of my characters. I had a male character called Doctor Temple, who plays a minor role in the first half of the story, but becomes more pivotal towards the end. When I was sending batches of chapters to my critique partner for feedback, she suggested it might be a good idea to change Doctor Temple from a man to a woman for a few reasons.

First, it brought more gender balance to the adult characters in the story, which was a brilliant suggestion and an oversight on my behalf. Second, changing the character to a woman would have a bigger emotional impact later in the story. Both were excellent suggestions, but, when I was still drafting, I kept the character as a man because I was over halfway through the book. Instead, I made a note to change the character's gender in the editing stage. I had planned to implement this change after the summer holiday break, but I forged ahead and did it early so the character was in the correct form before my next full read-through.

Another change I wanted to make was around my main character, Elliot. In her feedback, my Faber Academy tutor suggested I make some of his struggles more upfront and direct. This change involved an easy modification at the beginning of the book, so I also implemented it before the break.

## Enforced Break from Book

After completing these changes and many smaller tweaks, I felt that the book was in a good place to rest for the summer. The timing worked out very well, as, once my children's school finished for the summer holiday, the time I could have spent on the book would have been limited in any case.

Having a break between drafting and major editing and revisions is always a good idea. It gives you some separation from the story, which lets you tackle the edits with a clear mind.

That said, I found taking time away from the book difficult. I was itching to start on the major revisions. When I went on my summer holiday that year, I also had to stop myself from loading a version of the novel onto my Kindle. I knew full well I'd be tempted to read it beside the hotel swimming pool.

As much as I tried not to think about the first draft, I did, and I had several ideas to push the manuscript forward. I made note of those ideas and then tried to forget them for a few weeks.

The school holidays lasted six weeks and I managed five before returning to work on the manuscript. My wife and children left for a last-minute getaway with my sister-in-law and nieces. As the husbands were not going, I had the house to myself for the week. It would have been a shame not to take advantage of it.

## Full Read Through

My first task was to print out the book in its current state as a double-spaced manuscript, sit down with a red pen and start reading from start to finish. This was, I realised, the first time I had read the book all the way through.

Once I finished it, I was thrilled with how the story held together. Throughout the drafting stage, I had worked with an editor who gave me a professional opinion on the story and a good line edit. So, the manuscript, as it stood, was in relatively good shape, but there were some big issues I had to address.

## Structural Changes

First, I wanted to look at any structural changes. Because I had stayed close to my original beat sheet, the structure of the story didn't need a huge amount of work.

The first major change I needed to make was around the agency of my main character, Elliot. The Mars colony he lives in is quite regimented, so there is heavy adult influence. My course tutor commented that Elliot needs to drive more of the story, as opposed to being reactive to what's going on around him.

From my initial read-through, I could see what my tutor meant, so I still had to identify sections of the story that could be usefully changed, as well as write new scenes. Of all the structural changes, this was the most complex, and I spent a few weeks making it. But the work was worth it; I learned a big lesson about how important it is to have the protagonist drive the story, which I will remember for the sequel.

Another change I made was to balance the clues into the story's unfolding mystery. Sometimes I came too close to revealing what might happen in the finale, so I had to stagger the clues carefully. This sounds like a simple change, but it actually involved going through the manuscript in detail. Fortunately, I had made quite a few notes about balancing clues at the stage when I read through my entire manuscript for the first time.

Another change I made was around Mei, my sidekick character and Elliot's best friend. While she is important to the narrative, her story wasn't as developed as that of Elliot or the class bully Dimitri. Mei is portrayed as very headstrong and confident when she is with Elliot in the New London colony, but I deepened her character to reveal some struggles she faced with class members from her own school in New Beijing. That opened up a more vulnerable side of her character, which was great fun to write and helped me develop some ideas I can explore further in the sequel.

The last change I made at this stage was to reorder certain chapters. As with any science fiction story, I needed to work out the balance between story pace and rich world-building. I am proud of my world-building—and it was fun imagining football matches on Mars. There were some sequences early in the story where Elliot encounters a suspicious man near the colony hospital. I shifted this sequence a couple of chapters earlier. I felt this change worked well, as it was pivotal to the story, so I decided it would be better happening sooner. The move was straightforward, but there were a few details that had to be tidied up to avoid continuity problems.

I spent four weeks on these heavier structural changes, but I wasn't working on the book full time. I was averaging a couple of hours a day, mostly in the evening. While these changes took effort, working with a predefined beat sheet helped me maintain a straight and consistent structure, so in the grand scheme of the story, my changes were minor improvements to what was already there. I feel that having a beat sheet was a good move for me.

## Cutting Word Count

Now that my main structural changes were complete, I was left with a manuscript that was just over 80,000 words. If this had been an adult novel, that's a reasonable word count. For a middle-grade book, however, it felt too long. Science fiction and fantasy books have more leeway in terms of length as they require substantial world-building, but I felt more comfortable with the idea of a word count of 70,000 or lower.

During my first read-through, I identified some scenes and chapters that, while fun, added little to the story overall, so I marked them for removal. It's always difficult removing scenes, but the story felt much stronger for it. Some scenes I could delete without hesitation; others, I was still attached to, but the pace clearly picked up when they were removed. For example, in one series of chapters, the main characters and their families take a long rover trip to a colony dome called Paradise, which is a holiday centre with a water park—hey, it's a kids' book; they're allowed to have water slides on Mars. It's a fun sequence and, at its end, my main character encounters a mysterious man he met earlier in the story, triggering a key action scene that raises the story to a new level of threat and conflict. I still love these scenes, but I removed them and integrated the action sequence into another scene. This change saved me nearly 4,000 words in the manuscript. I still want to use this removed scene, but I've thought of a much better place for it in the sequel. It will be a much stronger scene there. I just hope I don't have to cut it again.

Once I had made these larger cuts, I worked through other scenes and trimmed the fat. In some places, I had too much description that, while rich, needed to be briefer. At this stage, I was digging into the fine detail and making numerous minor cuts. When this stage of editing was over, I had reduced the word count to 68,000 words, which felt like a much better length.

## Technical Edits (Tone, Voice, Mannerisms)

The next stage of my editing process was to focus on technical edits for overall tone, character voice and mannerisms. I knew I had an enormous problem to address, and I wasn't looking forward to tackling it.

When I received the extensive notes back from my Faber Academy course tutor for my first 15,000 words of the novel, there was one piece of very good yet tough feedback—the descriptive writing, as well as my main character's thoughts and dialogue, were a little too advanced for middle grade. This feedback came from a very experienced young adult and middle-grade author, so I paid attention.

My tutor suggested that I had a decision to make. Did I want to keep the book aimed at middle-grade, which suited my subject material, themes and plot well, or push it up to young adult? As I was partly writing this book for my son, who was ten at the time I published *Diary of a Martian*, I wanted to keep the book as middle-grade.

When I received that feedback on the first 15,000 words, I was about halfway through my draft. So, I decided I wouldn't go back and re-edit the first half of the book. Instead, from the halfway point, I made a conscious decision to soften the descriptive language and my characters' actions, dialogue and thoughts. I also let my critique partner know of this change as I submitted batches of chapters to her.

I was happy with the overall tone I adopted and very grateful for my tutor's advice, but this change left me with a manuscript with two distinct styles. The tone of the first half did not match that of the second. There was nothing for it. I had to start at the beginning, work my way through the chapters and adapt my writing style to match the second half of the book.

This substantial job took me a few weeks, but the resulting manuscript read much better. The work was worth it, and it was an immense weight off my mind to know that I now had a consistent tone throughout the book. I also learned a huge lesson here. Seek out feedback from people who know what they are talking about, hide your ego and listen to and adopt their suggestions, whether these come from a course tutor, beta reader or an experienced editor. Their advice and suggestions are worth their weight in gold.

With all the tonal changes complete, I had another aspect of my characters to look at: physical mannerisms. A few weeks before, I had seen a YouTube video on writing craft in which the interviewee explained how physical mannerisms are an effective way to add a little depth to a character. Let me give an example of how I implemented this. There are several places in my book where the school bully, Dimitri, is just nasty to my main character. When he is about to be mean, I added some details, like a click of the bone in his jaw or the crack of his knuckles. These small habits and physical mannerisms help to bring a character to life and, as readers recognise these actions, it helps them feel as though they are getting to know the characters.

For my secondary character, Mei, there were several mannerisms I wanted to add to the story. In moments of confidence, she waves her hands around in excitement. When she is angry and tells someone off, she has a habit of pointing her finger. In one scene, she stands up to Dimitri and pokes him in the chest, which catches him off guard. In contrast to her confident mannerisms, when she feels vulnerable or nervous, she has a tendency to play with strands of her hair. These actions and habits are subtle and were easy to add to the book, but I think they give a little more depth to the characters.

## Search for Personal Writing Ticks

My non-fiction writing experience had already made me aware of some of my bad writing habits, or ticks, as I like to call them. My biggest offenders are the words 'just', 'also' and 'started'. For this stage of self-editing, I targeted these specifically. To do this, I simply did a full document search in Scrivener to highlight each instance of the word and then checked if their use was justified. For example, when I found 'Elliot jumped up and started running towards the door', I changed it to 'Elliot jumped up and ran towards the door'. The word 'started' is my worst habit of all, so it was important that I started to remove them from the book. See what I did there? Moving on…

## Detailed ProWritingAid Checks

By this stage, I had been in the self-editing trenches for quite a while, knocking my manuscript into shape. I was now ready for the last checks before sending the entire book out to my editor.

For many years, I have used ProWritingAid, which is an advanced grammar and style checker. It's like the spelling and grammar checker in your favourite word processor, but turbo charged. There are many similar tools on the market, like Grammarly and Hemingway, but I enjoy using ProWritingAid, as I find it easy and intuitive to use. With every writing project I embark on, whether a book, blog post or article, I run it through ProWritingAid when I think I am finished. The process inevitably unearths many minor problems.

At this final stage of the novel, I wanted to make sure I eliminated as many problems as I could before sending the manuscript to my editor. You may think, Isn't that the editor's job? And it is, but I would rather an editor spend time resolving big issues in the story and not chasing after typos and misplaced commas. There is only so much time they can spend on a manuscript, so it's a good idea to get rid of any silly mistakes ahead of time.

My process at this stage is to work chapter by chapter and copy the text into ProWritingAid. First, I run the basic grammar report and work through any suggestions it makes, such as missing commas, passive voice or typos.

The following screenshot shows you what the general grammar report looks like. On the right side of the screen is a dropdown menu where you can select a writing style or genre.

This gives the tool a hint about what you are writing so that it can adapt itself accordingly. (It's very clever.) Below the drop-down menu are a series of sliders relating to different metrics, such as grammar and spelling, style and sentence length. The further to the right those markers are on the slider the better shape your writing is in. On the sliders is a grey bar that represents a range of acceptance. The marker doesn't have to be all the way to the right, as personal style can overrule convention, but if the marker is anywhere in that range, then you're doing okay.

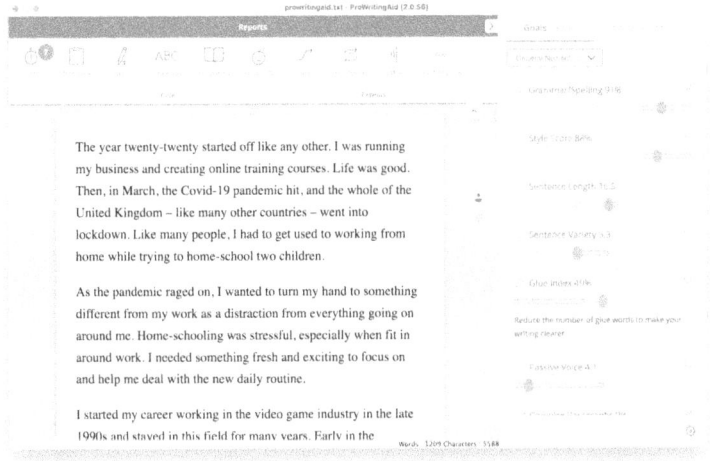

Editing with ProWritingAid

Once I have fixed everything in the general grammar report, I click on the grammar button on the toolbar, which runs a more advanced report (shown in the image below). If you felt good about fixing everything in the general grammar report, this report will probably reduce you to tears, but if you work through it and fix most of the issues, your writing will be the better for it.

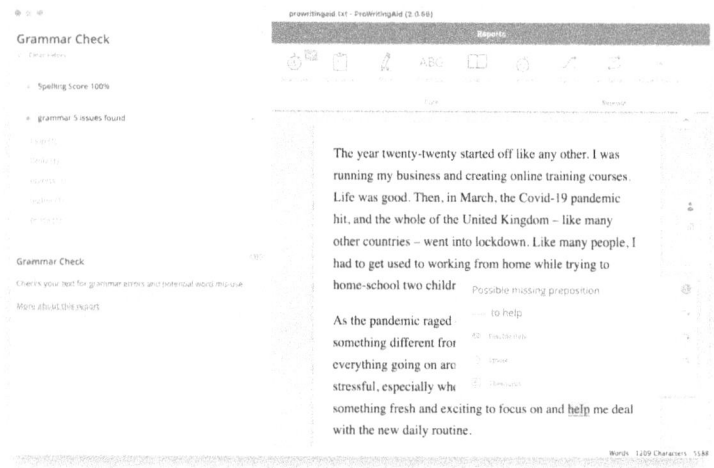

ProWritingAid Advanced Grammar Report

Once I have worked through the advanced grammar report, I click on the style button on the toolbar. The style checker (see image below) looks deeper into your writing for emotional telling, passive voice, adverbs and other stylistic issues. You don't have to fix everything in this report, as the suggestions are mainly a matter of style, but this report provides fantastic guidance for squashing adverbs, if that is what you want to do. Adverb use is a personal preference, and it's impossible to remove them all, but this report highlights excessive examples.

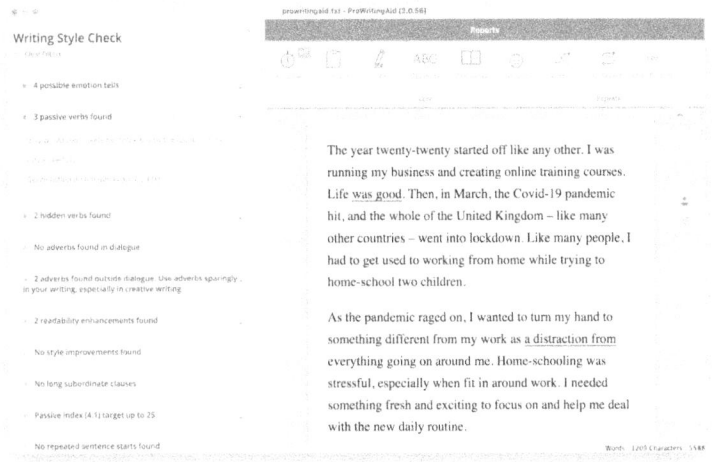

ProWritingAid Style Report

Once I have worked through each of these reports for each chapter, I am ready to package up the manuscript and send it off to a professional editor. At this stage, I can breathe a massive sign of relief, because the end is in sight.

## Key Takeaways

Reaching the first draft stage of a novel is only one small part of the writing process. The editing process can take a significant amount of time. If you outline your novel before writing, you are front-loading much of the structural work, which makes editing a little easier. People who are pure pantsers have told me that their editing process is harder because they have to reign in the structure. If you're a pantser, that's fine! Just remember the edit may be harder—not always but often.

With *Diary of a Martian* self-edited, I was feeling good about the project. The story hung together very well and I was a little shocked that I had a book I liked. Of course, I may look back at the novel in ten years and wonder, 'What were you thinking?' But, for now, I love it.

I will admit though, at this stage, I was tired. Even though I love the story, I was getting tired of reading it. I expect when the book is finally complete, I will be utterly sick of it. I hope that, as the years pass, I might enjoy reading it again without being reminded of all the work it took to get to this stage.

NINETEEN

# Working With a Professional Editor

Many years ago, I released several non-fiction books without using a professional editor. I regretted it. My readers reported typos—typos that I missed in self-editing. I missed them because it is very hard to spot all the typos in your own work, as you are so close to the project.

When I listen to podcasts or read interviews with authors—mostly self-published authors—who write five or more books a year and claim to not use editors because they are clean writers, I'm curious. So, I go onto Amazon and read the 'Look Inside' preview, or if they have published the book on Kindle Unlimited (Amazon's subscription book borrowing service), I read the first ten to twenty percent of the book. While some authors can genuinely write clean prose, more often than not, I spot numerous typos, grammar issues and general craft problems—issues that would be spotted, corrected or advised on by a professional editor or proofreader.

As an author, you need to decide what you want to do—hire an editor or not. It's your choice, and there are numerous factors to consider, cost being the largest. In my humble opinion, I feel it's a cost worth paying, because, if you ensure quality, any book you release has the potential to earn you an income for many years to come. As novels don't go out of date, I feel it's a good idea to make the initial upfront investment that gives some quality assurance to your hard work. That's my view anyway, and it's the route I took with *Diary of a Martian*.

Hiring an editor—especially a good one—can be expensive, but if you are serious about writing and publishing books, especially as a business, then ensuring you release high-quality books is very important. This is especially true in self-publishing, which already has a stigma of inferior quality. Some of my favourite books are from self-published authors and, in many cases, it's impossible to tell them apart from books published by a larger traditional publisher. Why? Because they have been professionally edited and proofread, and their covers and interior formatting look attractive and professional. Presentation matters, and that begins with the quality of the writing.

I have worked with many editors over the years and most have been excellent. But you need to find an editor who is a good fit for you. If, for example, you send your epic science fiction space opera to an editor who specialises in romantic fiction, you may not have a great experience. At the line- and copy-edit levels, the editor's specialisation shouldn't matter much. Still, you want to work with an editor who likes and knows your chosen genre, as you are likely to receive much better advice.

Some editors are open to editing a wide variety of genres, but it's always a good idea to check their interests and specialisations. You may not want to send your paranormal erotic romance full of randy werewolves to an editor who specialises in Christian fiction. Well, check with them first, at least.

## Types of Professional Editing

Editorial services come in many forms: developmental editing, line editing, copy editing, proofreading and sensitivity editing. You can hire someone to implement each stage, but, in reality, you may hire one editor for developmental as well as line and copy edits and then perhaps another editor for the proofreading stage. Let's take a quick look at the different editorial types and how they may apply to your work.

**Developmental Editing**: Developmental editing takes a high-level look at your story. Does the story make sense? Is it well structured? If you are writing in a specific genre, does it hit the expected tropes? Developmental editing isn't concerned with line-level grammar or style checks but with the high-level flow of the story and its structure.

**Line Editing**: The vast majority of editors that you hire will offer line-editing services. In this type of editing, the editor goes through your writing line by line and improves flow and efficiency by looking at word choice, removing redundancy and improving sentence structure. Line editing is often referred to interchangeably with copy editing, but it is actually different. That said, some editors, particularly freelance editors, will combine line- and copy-editing services.

**Copy Editing**: Compared to line editing, copy editing concerns smaller issues in a sentence. The editor goes through your writing line-by-line and checks for consistency in spelling and capitalisation, shifts in tense and similar grammatical details. Copy editing focuses on improving your writing by looking for inconsistencies and errors.

**Proofreading**: Proofreading is one of the final editing stages you can go through. Your final manuscript is sent for a last check to find any issues that may have sneaked past the line and copy editor. No matter how many experienced professionals have looked over your work, they are human, and it's possible for minor errors to creep through, particularly when they are also thinking about style and consistency. The proofreader focuses only on the accuracy of the grammar, spelling and punctuation. You can think of the proofreader as the last line of defence between you and your readers.

**Sensitivity Editing**: In the later stages, you can also hire a sensitivity editor or reader, whose job is to go through your book and make sure you don't have any biases or prejudices creeping into your work. For example, if you write about a social group different from your own, a sensitivity reader will make sure you use appropriate language and represent the group fairly. Their job isn't to do a line-by-line edit of your work but to look at what you are conveying as opposed to the technical aspects of your work.

## My Approach

For *Diary of a Martian*, I spent quite a lot of money on editing as I wanted to make sure this novel was as good as I could make it —especially as it's my first novel. In a previous chapter, I talked about how I paid an editor to act as a critique partner. I would bundle up three to five chapters at a time and send them to my editor to give me an honest critique of my work. This was a little like developmental editing, although the editor didn't have access to the entire story to assess, as I was submitting chapters as I wrote them. I used this approach to help me learn the craft and to stop me from veering off track.

Once I completed my self-editing phase, I sent the complete manuscript to the same editor. This time, she did a full line and copy edit of the document and offered advice on the story. This is a typical arrangement when hiring a freelance editor.

When you publish with a traditional publisher, you may work with a dedicated developmental editor first and then progress onto line and copy editing, but when hiring a freelancer, it is typical to combine these three roles to keep the costs lower. There are dedicated developmental editors you can hire if you wish, but this will increase your costs.

Once I received feedback from my editor, I spent about a week going over her changes and recommendations and implementing any required fixes. At this point, many of the changes were to help the prose flow better, which was an aspect of the manuscript I asked my editor to focus on. For me, if a reader—especially a young reader—has to reread a sentence or paragraph, I have failed with clarity.

After making revisions based on that feedback, I let the book sit for another week and didn't look at it. Then I read it through again to make sure I was happy with the book in its current state. Finally, I sent the book to an independent proofreader to get another expert to check for errors. I picked someone different for proofreading because they wouldn't be familiar with the story and would come at it with fresh eyes. Some editors have even told me that they will not do the final proofread of texts they have worked on in the earlier editing stages because it is hard to approach the text objectively.

In this phase of the book's development, I wasn't expecting

the proofreader to report any major issues, just to fix any typos that may have crept through and to ensure consistency at the line level. Plus, it was nice to have another professional look over my work, as, by this stage of the book's development, I wasn't sure if I could trust my opinion on the book anymore. I was too consumed by the project.

## Picking an Editor

There are many freelance editors available for hire who can work on just about any genre in existence and there are almost as many ways to pick and engage with them. When you are nearing the end of your first draft, start looking for an editor well ahead of time, because if you are hiring one directly, they will need to be booked in advance. It's quite rare to hire an editor who is available immediately, so I recommend looking a few months ahead of time (unless you are using an agency, which I will discuss in a moment). Let's look at a few options for hiring an editor.

**Word of Mouth**: You may already know other authors in person or via writing groups or internet forums. If you are looking to hire an editor, asking for personal recommendations from people who can vouch for an editor's quality is very helpful.

**Reading Book Credits**: You can also look at the copyright page in a book to see who edited it. If the book is traditionally published, it may not say, but if the book is independent, the author likely hired a freelancer and may have credited them. Find books you like and contact their editors for a price quote.

**Google**: Searching on Google or other search engines is another way to find an editor, although you won't have the benefit of a personal recommendation from another author or a book to guide you. When you search for an editor, their website should explain what types of books they edit, as well as anything they won't edit, such as extreme violence or erotica. Their website should also contain a list of books they have worked that you can check out to see if the editor might be a good fit.

If you find an editor you are interested in contacting, see if they offer a sample edit. Many editors allow you to send them up to 1,000 words or your book, and they will perform an edit for you to see their work. If they offer this, take them up on it. The type of edits they give you should tell you if they're someone you want to work with.

**Agencies**: Agencies are companies that will supply an editor to you on request. Two examples are Reedsy and Scribendi, among others. I haven't used Reedsy, but many writers swear by their author services, of which editing is one. What makes companies like Reedsy and Scribendi very useful is that they vet the editors. An editor can't just go to these companies and ask for work. They have to prove themselves to the companies first, so you know you are working with an experienced professional. They have to pass a series of editing tests and interviews, as well as have proven experience. Companies like Scribendi also have quality assurance systems to ensure that the editors are upholding the company standard. This extra layer of oversight is a further protection to authors.

As I have not worked with Reedsy, I will explain how I work with Scribendi, which I have used for years. Once you have a document to be edited, you upload the document to their site. The word count is calculated, and you then select what type of job you want, such as editing or proofreading. You are then given a series of return dates and the related costs.

The faster you want the document back, the more it costs. Time frames can range from two hours for a short document to several weeks for a book-length project. Once you pick the time frame you want, you can write a message to the editor highlighting any areas of your writing that you want them to focus on or any concerns you have. You pay upfront, and Scribendi then makes that document available to editors specialised in your type of project.

You then wait. When the editor has finished, they will return the documents to you with a high-level report and a couple of Word files with marginal comments—more on this later in the chapter.

If you like that editor's work, you can use their editor code next time to request the same person. If you don't specify an editor next time, you will end up with someone else, which is what I did for blog posts and older book projects. With *Diary of a Martian*, I liked the feedback I received when I was using my editor as a critique partner, so I selected the same person when line editing the whole novel and this book.

## Costs

I will not sugar-coat it. Hiring an experienced editor is expensive, and how much you pay is up to you. I can't tell you if you should spend the money or not, but I will say that an editor can make your book shine. Having a trained professional work with you is the best way to ensure that you release a high-quality book. However, you may pay anywhere from $1000 to $3000 (or more) to have your book edited and proofread.

If the idea of spending that amount worries you—and I understand why—think of it this way. If you believe in your book, want to release it and have people buy it, you need to think of that book as a valuable asset. That may sound corporate, but the truth is, if you release your book intending for people to buy it, you need to think of it as a product.

If spending that much on an editor isn't workable, don't fret. As an alternative, I recommend purchasing software like ProWritingAid and Grammarly and making good use of it. You might also ask as many people as you know to help proofread your book. There are also many books on the market that help authors with the self-editing process, that you can work through.

Freelancer sites, like Fiverr and Upwork, are another place to hire editors, but be careful; if someone offers to edit a 70,000 book for only $200, it's wise to ask yourself why it's such a paltry sum. It may be a case of getting what you pay for. I know some editors on these platforms will simply run your book through ProWritingAid to perform a grammar check. You can do that yourself.

## Ways of Working

The many editors I've worked with over my career all seem to operate in a similar style. You send them a document to be edited; typically, this will be in Microsoft Word format, using 12-point Times New Roman font and double spacing. Not all editors are strict about this format, but it's an industry standard. I use Scrivener as my day-to-day word processor, but, for editing, I export my novel using the processor's manuscript template, which defaults to the industry standard.

When the editor has completed the work, you will receive

back a few files. The first is a high-level report in which the editor tells you what is working and what isn't in your writing, including any bad habits you need to look at. This report gives you a good overview of the editor's opinion. You will also receive two Word files: one containing every single change that the editor has made, such as fixing typos and small modifications, and a second with all those smaller changes approved and the remaining larger editorial comments presented in the margins. The second is the crucial document to look at as it will contain all the issues you need to address.

In terms of your editor changing your manuscript, you need to be upfront about what you want your editor to do. Some writers don't like anyone changing their text and would rather just be told in comments about what the issues are, although this makes the editor's job more difficult.

By default, an editor will perform line-level corrections and make suggestions about larger issues that need to be addressed. When I work with my editor at Scribendi, I state that I'm happy for her to make any changes she sees fit. If two sentences would be better merged into one and it's easier to just do it rather than explain it, I am happy for that to happen. If a change like that is made, she will leave a marginal comment, suggesting that I check the edit. Be clear with your editor about the changes you are happy for them to make. This makes the editing process easier for both of you.

Once you've received the edits, your job as a writer is to work through the editor's comments and make any changes you choose. You don't have to do everything an editor suggests. It's your book, so you can decide not to adopt a suggestion. However, remember that the editor is a professional with experience, so if they suggest something, there is probably a good reason. I will accept ninety-nine percent of my editor's suggestions. I might not agree with something, but this is rare.

It can take a long time to go through every comment made by an editor on a full-length novel, but once you have, you will be left with a book of a higher standard.

## Editorial Nervousness

The first time you work with an editor, it's pretty terrifying. I remember the first book I had returned by an editor. When that email arrived, I broke out into a cold sweat. I could hardly open the email. It's only natural to be nervous, because you're allowing someone else to comment on and criticise your work. That's hard.

Remember one thing, though: the editor is on your side. They are professionals, and their job is to help you succeed. They want you to produce the best book you can, which is why an editor's critique can feel tough. I always tell myself that I would rather an editor find all the mistakes in private than a reader in public.

If you are working with an editor for the first time, I suggest approaching their reply as follows. First, read their summary report about the project. Absorb what they are saying. If there is a general problem in your writing, they will point it out here. If they highlight a problem, don't panic. Close the email, go for a walk and think about what they've said.

After a brief break, open up the file that has all the minor changes accepted and glance over the marginal comments. Don't fix anything yet. Just read the comments. This will give you a good idea of the work you might have ahead of you. If you feel good about what you are seeing, dive in and start fixing.

If some of the comments are tough and you feel a little upset, close the document and leave it for a day or two. Then, with a clear mind, tackle the changes.

Having worked with many editors over the years, I no longer

fear their feedback. Actually, I quite enjoy it, because I know that once I have implemented the changes, I will have a much stronger book.

The truth is, even the best authors may receive heavy edits on their writing. One editor I employed used to work for one of the big-five publishers. She told me about a client who was a hugely successful best-selling author—I won't divulge the name. She said that this author was brilliant at telling a compelling and exciting story, but the technical aspects of writing, such as efficiency and grammar, were not their strongest points. But, she explained, this was fine. The author was a superb storyteller, and it was the editor's job to help with the technical aspects of how the work was presented on the page. What she said has always stuck with me and the author in question has sold millions of books.

So, I'll say it again. The editor is there to offer their professional expertise to help you succeed, which is why I believe professional editing is an important part of the writing process and worth the cost. While it's a large amount of money to pay upfront, hopefully your book will have lasting appeal and remain on sale for years to come and, if its quality is high, you have a better chance of making sales and recouping your costs.

## Key Takeaways

Editorial feedback on your writing is hugely important. Many years ago, I made the mistake of releasing a couple of books without the help of an editor. To be honest, I couldn't afford one, but I paid the price for it through bad reviews that highlighted issues in the writing.

I now consider working with an editor a vital part of the process of creating a high-quality book. It is also easier to feel confident about releasing your book into the world when you know that at least one professional, if not two, has already looked over your work.

Try not to be intimidated by working with an editor. Editors are there to make you look good. Every editor I have ever worked with has been obsessed with books. They read loads, and their professional lives are focused on helping produce outstanding books. Many editors are also writers. And guess what they do with their own books … They hire independent editors to help them …

TWENTY

## Book Formatting

The writing for *Diary of a Martian* was complete, edited and proofread. It had taken a lot of work to get to that point, but it would be the next steps that would turn the text from a word processor into a finished book.

My intention was to self-publish the novel instead of going through a traditional publisher. This book won't be covering the publishing process itself—that's for another book—but I want to talk about the final few steps that put a finished book in your hands.

If you work with a traditional publisher, the formatting, marketing copy and cover design will be handled for you—sometimes with your input, often without. When self-publishing, you handle all these tasks.

### Print vs eBook

When publishing a book, you have several formats to manage to meet a reader's expectations. The primary formats are a paperback, hardback and eBook, such as for the Kindle, Kobo or any other e-reader device on the market.

**Print**: Even in this modern digital age, physical printed books remain very popular and both paperback and hardback books can be produced with ease. In the traditional publishing world, books are printed in bulk using a process called offset printing. These books are then stored in a warehouse and distributed to stores via a distribution company, such as Gardners.

Self-published physical books, known as digital printed books, are printed on demand. A customer orders a copy of the book via Amazon, for example. The book is then printed with a very high-end industrial-size laser or inkjet printer. The pages are cut to size, the printed cover is glued onto the book and the book is shipped to the customer.

The quality of print-on-demand books has increased over the years, and it is possible to create a top-quality, good-looking book with either a paperback or hardback cover. I would argue that if the book is well designed, it is, in fact, of higher quality than a traditional offset printed book, as offset printing uses very cheap and rough-textured paper.

I like to imagine a future where you walk into a physical bookshop on the high street, request a book—maybe a niche title—and, if it isn't in stock, they print and bind it for you while you drink a nice cup of tea in their cafe.

Even with the popularity of e-reading devices, such as the Kindle, many people still prefer to buy and read a physical book, so it's important to satisfy their needs when preparing your finished book.

. . .

***eBook***: Electronic reading devices have become very popular. Instead of buying a physical paperback, you can go to an online store, such as Amazon or Kobo, buy a book and have it delivered to your device within seconds, ready to read.

I bought my first e-reader, a Kindle, back in 2011, and I have been hooked ever since. E-readers can be quite controversial among hardcopy purists, but the reality is that, if you release books, a large proportion of your readers will use a device to read them.

I am a fairly avid reader. In 2022 alone, I have read nearly seventy-five books. All those books look great on a shelf, but I can't realistically store that many at home (according to my wife, at least).

These days, I read novels and nonfiction books on the Kindle and only purchase large, colour coffee-table books in physical copies. I enjoy books about the film-making process. These are large books packed with photos and paintings from a movie's preproduction. I buy and collect those books in hardback, but the rest of my books live in my Kindle library.

Giving your readers an option of how to read your book is vital and producing eBooks is easier than you might think. From a commercial point of view, the profit margins on eBooks can be quite high compared to the cost of producing physical books, especially if you are writing a long-running series.

One feature of eBooks and e-readers that I appreciate is the ability to change the text formatting and fonts of the book you're reading. On one occasion during the COVID-19 pandemic, I was flying to speak at a conference when you still had to wear face masks on a plane. It was a four-hour flight, and I just couldn't wear my glasses with a mask for that long. No matter what I tried, my glasses would steam up. In the end, I had to take them off, so I just increased the font size on my Kindle to continue reading on the flight.

A friend of mine loves reading but is dyslexic. On his Kindle, he really appreciates being able to change the font to one that's easier for him to read, such as a San-Serif typeface or the Open Dyslexia font. A Kindle has been transformational for his ability to enjoy fiction by changing the fonts and reducing the amount of text on the screen at any point.

E-readers have drawn criticism from people who prefer physical books, but they can be excellent for people with certain accessibility needs. Even if you don't like e-readers, I would urge you to consider them as assistive devices for people who may struggle to read from a physical book. There are many reasons readers might benefit from eBooks; they may need a larger or easier font or have weak wrists and struggle to hold a larger book. Support the eBook format, even if you don't like it. This gives readers a choice, and people love choice.

## DIY Book Formatting Options

Formatting can seem intimidating if you haven't done it before. However, there are many options for formatting your book that cater to different skill levels.

**Direct from Your Word Processor**: Most modern word processors, such as Microsoft Word, Apple Pages and Scrivener, offer tools to format your manuscript into a book and export a print-ready PDF. When I first dabbled with releasing my own books, I used Microsoft Word for formatting, but, while it was not complicated, I was never entirely happy with the result. It looked okay, perfectly passable, but nowhere near as good as traditionally published books.

It is possible to produce good-looking results using a word processor, but it can take a lot of fiddling. If you are not in a position to purchase additional tools or services, and you need to use what you already have, you can still produce a nice-looking book—just be prepared to spend a long time experimenting and tweaking.

To create an eBook, marketplaces like Amazon KDP allow you to upload a Word file onto their platform and handle the conversion into an eBook for you, which is very helpful. If you do not want to explore any other paid options for creating an eBook, then uploading the Word file is perfectly sufficient, but you do lose any control over the final formatting and appearance of your book.

**Custom Book Formatter Software**: To avoid fiddling with a word processor, a good solution is custom book-formatting software. The two market leaders are Vellum and Atticus. Vellum is an Apple Mac-only application and Atticus works on both Microsoft Windows and Apple Mac. Both applications offer similar features and are very good for their purposes.

To use them, you import a manuscript file containing the text of your book. The software then attempts to split your book into chapters based on the headings you set in the original document. You correct any errors until you have the desired structure for your book.

Next, you assign a formatting template to your book. This format will set the font for the body text and headings and add graphical flourishes for elements such as scene breaks and chapter headings. Then, you can tweak the format so the book suits your taste. These tweaks will apply to the entire book at once, making it quick and easy to experiment with layout and style. Once you are happy with the visual styles, you can export your book, which is now ready for publication.

Both Vellum and Atticus allow you to export a print-ready

PDF file for your physical paperback or hardback book and an ePub (generic eBook format) or mobi (eBook format used by Amazon) file to upload to eBook stores.

Tools like Vellum and Atticus make the book formatting process easy and fun. While there is a one-off cost associated with these tools (between $149 and $249), if you plan to write many books, the cost is justifiable over time, especially as hiring someone to format the book for you can cost as much.

***Professional Desktop Publishing***: Another option is to use industry-standard design and typesetting software to lay out your book. The most commonly used software package for this purpose is Adobe InDesign. With Vellum and Atticus, discussed above, you give up some control over the formatting and layout for ease of use. With InDesign, you have complete control over everything in your book, but the process is much more complicated.

While a non-designer can use InDesign with good results, the degree of effort will be significant. I tried to learn InDesign, but I struggled to get the book looking as I wanted it. The problem was definitely me and not InDesign, which is a professional and well-used tool, but the software package is clearly aimed at professional designers. If Vellum and Atticus give you ease of use over full control, then InDesign gives you full control over ease of use.

If you are publishing through a traditional publisher, or if you hire a professional book formatter, they will most likely use InDesign and the designers will be trained typesetters. Tools like Vellum and Atticus are perfect for self-published authors.

## Freelancer Options

If you don't like the thought of formatting the book yourself, you can hire a freelancer to do this for you and prices vary. For prices lower than $300, the formatter may use Vellum or Atticus to produce your book, which isn't a problem, but for a similar cost, you can buy the software and do it yourself. The higher-priced freelancers will most likely be using Adobe InDesign or an equivalent application.

I think hiring a freelancer to format your book is a completely valid thing to do. Formatting a book can be time consuming, even when using dedicated software tools. However, apart from cost, the big downside to hiring someone to format your book is flexibility. What happens if you need to make some changes?

For example, what if you find a mistake after the book is released and you want to upload your PDF or eBook file back to the stores? Well, I can tell you what happens: you pay your freelancer to make the changes for you. It may not be as expensive as the initial setup of the book, but you will most likely have to pay a small fee for their time.

## My Approach

I strongly favour the do-it-yourself approach to producing my books and I enjoy the process. I'm also a bit of a control freak with my projects, so I prefer to do as much as I can, unless the work ventures into territories where I am not skilled, such as editing and cover design.

I am a long-term user of Vellum, with which I have formatted many nonfiction titles, so I was looking forward to using it to produce a novel.

First, I had to decide what size of paperback to produce.

The standard size for most novels is 5x8 inches, which is what I configured. Once I imported the Word file containing my novel, I started playing with Vellum's many templates.

One template allows you to add a background image to the start of a chapter. I wanted a custom background featuring the planet Mars, so I purchased a stock photo image, cropped it to the correct size and loaded it into the template. You can see what this looks like in the following screenshot from Vellum with a preview of a page from the paperback version of my novel.

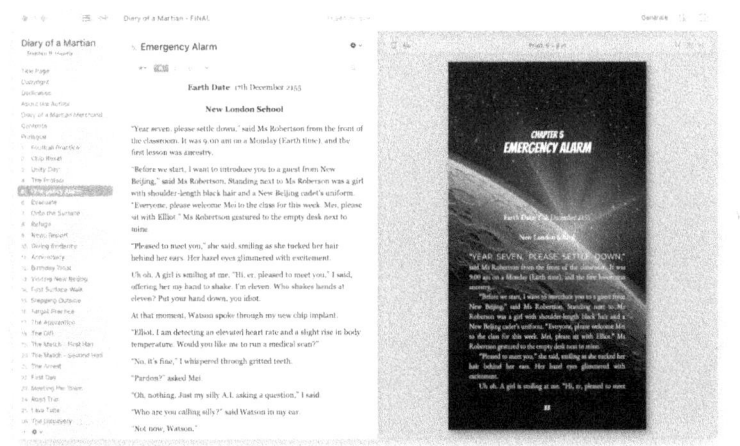

Vellum showing a paperback preview.

Once I had finished formatting the paperback version, I could see what the eBook version would look like, and I didn't really have to make any changes. The eBook version just worked, as you can see in the following screenshot.

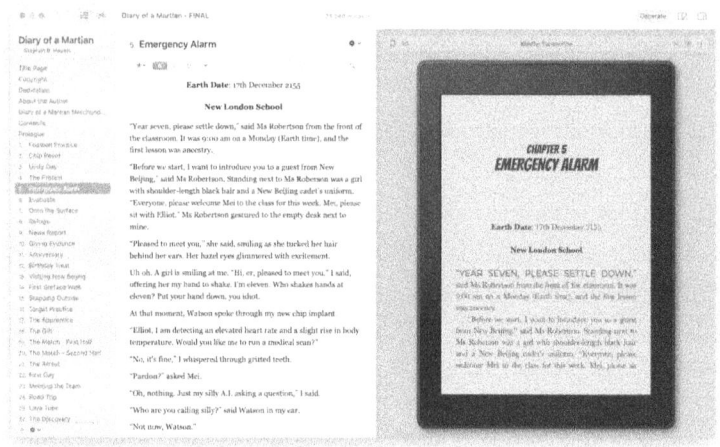

Vellum showing a Kindle preview.

Using Vellum, the formatting didn't take me too long—about four hours, and much of that was checking each page to ensure it looked right. I have used Vellum many times, so I already knew what I was doing. Still, I expect that even factoring in the learning curve of using the software for the first time, you will have a formatted book within a day.

I always enjoy the formatting process. It's very rewarding to see that double-spaced manuscript in 12 pt. Times New Roman font transform into a publishable book.

## Key Takeaways

It's hard to describe the feeling of moving from a finished manuscript to formatting the inside of the book. The book takes on a new life when you can visualise exactly what your readers will see.

There are many ways to approach the formatting of your book. The most versatile is to use software like Adobe InDesign, as you have control over every aspect of the page, but it is also the most complicated and requires a good eye for design, something that I don't have. Instead, I prefer using dedicated formatting software, like Vellum or Atticus. They give you enough creative control to get the look you want without requiring advanced design skills.

TWENTY-ONE

## Blurb Writing and Marketing Copy

With the manuscript formatted into a paperback and eBook, the next step was to write the back cover blurb and marketing text. I won't lie: for me, this was one of the hardest parts of the book-writing process. Finalising the blurb for the back cover took me weeks and weeks of writing, rewriting, soliciting feedback and more rewriting.

The back-cover blurb is only one piece of the marketing copy that needs to be written. In this chapter, I talk about my tag line, log line, back-cover blurb, selling paragraph and call to action. Each of these pieces of marketing copy is important when selling and promoting a book to your readers.

### Log Line and Tag Line

The tag and log lines are brief, but essential. A tag line is a short piece of text, usually a single line, used to convey a brand message. The log line is a brief statement that summarises your story. You can imagine how difficult it was to distil over 70,000 words down to a few sentences. First, let's look at some examples of tag lines from popular brands:

Just Do It.
*Nike*

Melts in your mouth, not in your hands.
*M&M*

Redbull gives you wings.
*Redbull*

The happiest place on Earth.
*Disney Land*

There is probably a good chance you have heard the tag lines for these popular brands and when you hear them, you instantly know what they represent. In just a few words, they conjure up a powerful image in your mind. As writers, we want to do the same thing—capture the book's essence in a few words. There have been some fantastic book tag lines, such as:

Bind your fate to mine.
*Lore* by Alexandra Bracken

Half boy. Half god. All Hero.
*Percy Jackson and the Lightning Thief* by Rick Riordan

Champions are not born. They're made.
*Ashlords* by Scott Reintgen

Could you murder your wife to save your daughter?
*Her Last Tomorrow* by Adam Croft

At just twelve years old, Artemis Fowl is a criminal genius.
*Artemis Town* by Eoin Colfer

You think you're safe ... But I know what you did.
*When I Find You* by Emma Curtis

With examples like these in mind, I set out to write a tag line for my book. It took a few attempts. My first attempt was:

A chance discovery on Mars answers one of humanity's biggest questions. Are we alone in the universe?

This tag line was based on the original twenty-five-word pitch that I wrote at the start of the project, which was, 'When Martian colonists discover a doorway in a hidden tunnel, humanity can finally answer one of its biggest questions: Are we alone in the universe?' While I like the pitch, it felt a little flat as a tag line, and feedback from other writers in writing forums and my critique partner suggested the same.

In the end, I landed on:

Football, friends and ... extra-terrestrials? Just another day on Mars.

I like this tag line as it conveys a few important points about the story. First, the main character is a normal kid. He plays football and hangs out with his friends, which anchors the reader in a kid's reality. Then, we add the element of extra-terrestrials. It's a sci-fi story and we're going on an adventure. Finally, I remind the reader that we are on Mars. The tag line is deceptively short, but it took immense effort. Don't think you can just write a few words and call it a day. Experiment with a wide variety of lines and get feedback from other people.

Next, I needed to write a log line. As a brief statement about or summary of a story, the log line is less about a branding message than about giving a sense of the narrative itself. You might ask yourself: If I had to describe my story in one tweet on Twitter, what would I write?

You can use the log line when discussing your book with other people who ask about the story—a bit like a classic elevator pitch—or as marketing text with a paid social media advert. My intention was for my log line to build on the tag line. After several attempts, I ended up with the following log line:

Between football games and bullies, living on Mars seems a lot like living on Earth. That is, until twelve-year-old Elliot makes a discovery that may hold the key to one of humanity's biggest questions: Are we alone in the universe?

You'll notice that it's quite similar to the tag line, but expanded. We first get a grounding in Elliot's reality—he has to deal with normal occurrences like football and dealing with bullies. We also learn his name and age, which helps to attract the target audience. Finally, in the mention of humanity's biggest question, we understand that this is a sci-fi story that leads the reader on a momentous adventure.

## Book Blurb

Next, I needed to write the back cover description for the book, otherwise called the book blurb. When a potential reader picks up a book from the shelf, they will make two quick decisions. First, do they like the cover? As much as people say you shouldn't judge a book by its cover, that's exactly what happens.

Second, are they grabbed by the back cover or the description on the online store?

The book description can make or break someone's decision to buy your book. I know how important it is, and, if I'm honest, I was scared of this part of the process. I probably should have put thought into the blurb much earlier, but I put it off as long as I could. The blurb felt much harder to write than the book itself.

I began the process by collecting blurbs from some comparable books. Here are a few examples from *Artemis Fowl*, *Harry Potter and the Philosopher's Stone* and *Percy Jackson and The Lightning Thief*.

**"AT JUST TWELVE YEARS OLD, ARTEMIS FOWL IS A CRIMINAL GENIUS.**

No scheme is too dastardly, no plot too devious. And he's just discovered that fairies are real.

Poor fairies.

But these are not the cuddly creatures of bedtime stories. They are armed. They are dangerous. And when Artemis captures Captain Holly Short for her fairy gold, he messes with the wrong elf.

Holly isn't armed but she's *incredibly* dangerous, and pretty annoyed with all the kidnapping.

Artemis Fowl is about to find out that fairies fight back ."

*"Turning the envelope over, his hand trembling, Harry saw a purple wax seal bearing a coat of arms; a lion, an eagle, a badger and a snake surrounding a large letter 'H'.*

Harry Potter has never even heard of Hogwarts when the letters start dropping on the doormat at number four, Privet Drive. Addressed in green ink on yellowish parchment with a purple seal, they are swiftly confiscated by his grisly aunt and uncle. Then, on Harry's eleventh birthday, a great beetle-eyed giant of a man called Rubeus Hagrid bursts in with some astonishing news: Harry Potter is a wizard, and he has a place at Hogwarts School of Witchcraft and Wizardry. An incredible adventure is about to begin!"

---

**"Look, I didn't want to be a half-blood. I never asked to be the son of a Greek God.**

I was just a normal kid, going to school, playing basketball, skateboarding. The usual. Until I accidentally vaporized my maths teacher. Now I spend my time battling monsters and generally trying to stay alive."

---

While I wasn't looking to emulate these blurbs, they served as a great inspiration for how to write the back cover material. Initially, I really liked that the Percy Jackson blurb was written from a first-person point of view. My first attempt at a blurb was also written in the first-person voice of my protagonist. I was quite happy with it, but, in various writing groups and internet forums, everyone seemed to hate it and it sparked a massive debate about whether we should write blurbs from the first-person perspective or not.

I wasn't looking to start a debate; I was just looking for feedback. So, if it caused that much grief, I needed to change it. If you're curious about what that first attempt looked like, here it is:

**"I'm Elliot and I'm twelve years old. I'm also a Martian. I don't have green skin or bug eyes though. I look just like a regular kid on Earth.**

I live in the New London colony at the base of the Olympus Mons volcano.

Life on Mars for a twelve-year-old is tough!

At school, I spend a lot of time avoiding the class bully and his wedgies.

You can't just go outside to hang out with your friends either. Everything about this planet wants to hurt you.

My life changes when I start work experience with our planet engineers. When out on a routine survey mission, where I finally get to go outside, I make a discovery that will change our lives forever.

Are we alone in the universe? Let's find out!"

I spent several weeks tinkering with a new blurb written in the third-person and, after receiving lots of feedback from other writers and finally my editor, I settled on the following:

**"Elliot's a Martian. Although you wouldn't know it – he's just like a regular kid from Earth … except he was born on Mars.**

Life in a Martian colony can be tough for a twelve-year-old! You can't just go outside to hang out because, well, you'd suffocate and die.

Elliot lives a regular Martian life. He goes to school, plays football, and tries to avoid the mean kids. But he never gets to leave the colony buildings. That is, until he goes on a science trip where he makes a discovery that could change the course of humanity forever: a strange doorway in a volcanic cave! Who put it there? What's on the other side?

Join Elliot and his friends as their lives go from the ordinary to the extraordinary. The solar system as we know it will never be the same again."

I'm thrilled with the final blurb, but when I write the sequel to *Diary of a Martian*, I will start the blurb-writing process much earlier. So much rides on the blurb, which I found stressful. My best bit of advice is to not write a blurb in isolation. This is what your readers will see first, and, if it's not effective, it might be the only part of your book they read. To make sure it makes them want to read more, seek out as much feedback as you can, especially from your editor.

You will notice that my tag line, log line and blurb build on each other. The log line builds on the tag line, and the blurb builds on the log line. This is deliberate. The log line, tag line and blurb should work together to describe your book and brand, helping the reader make an informed buying decision.

## Selling Paragraph

The next piece of marketing text to write is the selling paragraph. This paragraph won't appear on the back of the book but, instead, with the blurb on website sales pages, such as Amazon, Waterstones or Barnes and Noble.

The aim of the selling paragraph is to reinforce, for the buyer, who the book is for and which books it is similar to. Here is the selling paragraph I wrote for *Diary of a Martian*:

> "*Diary of a Martian* is the first book in a series for fans of action, adventure and science fiction. If you like Harry Potter, Artemis Fowl or Percy Jackson, then you'll love this series that combines fast-paced action, down-to-earth characters and settings that are out of this world. Perfect for younger readers and adults to enjoy."

Let's break it down.

> "*Diary of a Martian* is the first book in a series for fans of action, adventure and science fiction."

First, I am telling the reader that this is the first in a series; it's not a stand-alone book. Also, the reader should like the book if they like action, adventure and science fiction. The reader now knows explicitly what the genre of the book is and what they can expect: action and adventure.

> "If you like Harry Potter, Artemis Fowl or Percy Jackson, then you'll love this series that combines fast-paced

action, down-to-earth characters and settings that are out of this world."

Next, I am making direct comparisons. If you like Harry Potter, Artemis Fowl or Percy Jackson, you should enjoy this book. Not only is this guidance for the reader, it also helps with search engine optimisation when buyers search for books on websites like Amazon, because, at its core, Amazon is a search engine for products. The comparisons to Harry Potter and the other characters can be swapped out if I come across other books that offer better comparisons. I expect that I will tweak those names several times after the launch.

"Perfect for younger readers and adults to enjoy."

Finally, I reaffirm that this is a book for younger readers, but that adults may enjoy it too. Middle-grade books are quite popular with adult readers, as they are easy, fast-paced and good fun, without all the seriousness of adulthood—in other words, a great escape from the worries of real life. Well, that's why I enjoy them, anyway.

## Call to Action

The last piece of marketing copy I had to write is the call to action (CTA), which is an instruction to the reader that prompts them to buy the book. It sounds simple, but many product marketing materials miss this part. The CTA urges the reader to take action. Of course, not everyone will take this call to action, but it would surprise you how effective it can be.

Think about all those YouTube videos that tell you to 'Smash that like button and ring the bell'. That's a CTA. You are being asked to take an action and the YouTube channels are hoping you will subscribe.

In my case, I will use the CTA in social media marketing campaigns, as well as after the selling paragraph on online product pages. My CTA is simple:

"Buy this book to start your Martian adventure!"

Simple yet effective. Want to go on a Martian adventure? Buy this book. The structure of a sales page is simple. In my case, I will have the log line to draw the reader in with a very high-level summary. The blurb will hook them into the setting, characters and story. Next, the selling paragraph will confirm the book's audience and genre. Finally, the CTA will ask them to buy the book.

## Key Takeaways

Writing the marketing copy for a book is very hard. The log line, tag line, blurb, selling paragraph and CTA exist for one purpose alone: to sell your book. Many writers, myself included, find this the least enjoyable part of the entire book production process, but it's essential if you want people to read your book. Marketing and sales are hard, but if you want to succeed, no matter how you publish your book, you need to give a lot of attention to the marketing copy.

If you work with a traditional publisher, parts of the marketing copy will be handled for you, although when I have been traditionally published, I still had to write my own blurbs.

While crucial, the marketing copy is only part of the package you present to convince readers to buy your book. The next stage in the process is the book cover design … because whether you like it or not, your book will be judged by its cover.

TWENTY-TWO

## Cover Design

With the marketing copy written, I needed to concentrate on the book cover. I have minimal skills in artwork and graphic design, so I knew I would have to use a freelancer who specialises in book covers. I strongly recommend never doing your own book covers (unless you are a graphic designer) if you have the means. Hire a professional who specialises in them. The results will be much better.

For *Diary of a Martian*, I had an end goal in mind. I didn't want a cover that stands out too much; instead, I wanted one that fits with my genre. Readers can be creatures of habit, and, if you try to stand out too much, you risk being overlooked.

### Series Logo

The first part of my plan was to have a series logo designed. At a minimum, I intend *Diary of a Martian* to be a trilogy. The first book stands on its own as a story with a clear resolution at the end, but I have an arc planned that spans three books. No matter what happens, I plan to release the whole trilogy. If there is further demand, I can expand the story. With this plan, I wanted a logo that would be common across all the books.

For a sense of what I mean, think about the Star Wars logo. Currently, there are three trilogies and many stand-alone films and TV series, but you can instantly tell they are all Star Wars because of that simple but effective yellow text-based logo 'Star Wars'. This is what I wanted: a logo that is simple but memorable.

I had a few options. I could hire a freelance logo designer from a company like Fiverr, which was the cheapest option, or I could run a design competition using the company 99designs. A design competition enables you to receive lots of design options from different designers. You then whittle those designs down to three or four finalists and work with the designers to tweak the designs. You then pick a winning design, and that designer wins the design prize money. Running a competition is more expensive than hiring a freelancer to create a single logo, but, with the contest, you will have many logo options to choose from, so that's the approach I took.

I set up the competition to run over a one-week period. In my brief to the contestants, I noted that I wanted a simple logo that said 'Diary of a Martian' and used the Star Wars and Star Trek logos as examples. I launched the competition and waited for the entries to flood in, and flood in they did. I had seventy logo concepts to choose from. The results were amazing, which also made it very hard to choose one.

First, I removed all the logos that didn't leap out at me. Many logos looked too childish, and they were rejected. Even though the book is a middle-grade novel, quite a few logos looked better suited to five- to eight-year-olds.

It didn't take me long to whittle down the choices to ten logos. I then solicited feedback from family, friends and anyone who would listen. This helped me narrow down my options to four. I took those designers into the final round of the competition. The designers and I spent a few days refining the concepts and I then had to pick a winner.

In all honesty, I would have been happy with any of the finalists. The designs were all excellent, but I could only pick one winner, which you see below.

Diary of a Martian Logo.

I loved the simplicity of the typeface, which communicated science fiction. The curved underline evoked the curve of Mars. While in its raw form the logo is a single-colour vector image, any cover designer I hire can add their own texturing to the logo, which will give the cover designer flexibility with how they use the logo, as long as it's consistent across the series.

## Book Cover Design

Armed with my new logo, I now needed to find a designer to work with. There are several options for a cover, and that which you choose depends heavily on the expectations for your chosen genre. It's important to identify books comparable to your own and choose a cover option that fits with them. The cover styles you can choose are vector-based illustrations, stock library montages or custom illustrations.

**Vector-Based Illustration**: Vector illustrations are covers that have been designed using a vector-based art package, such as Adobe Illustrator. This style of cover is very popular with romantic comedies or cosy mysteries. The covers are quite simple and colourful.

**Stock Library Montage**: Another popular option is a montage of stock photo images. A good example might be a thriller cover in which the protagonist is running into the distance, set against an interesting cityscape. These covers are built by purchasing stock photo images, cutting out the relevant pieces and blending them together in Photoshop. Many genres use this form, especially thrillers, mysteries and police procedurals.

**Custom Illustration**: The other option is to have a digital artist paint a custom illustration and design the cover around that illustration and the cover text. Here, you might have what looks like a digital oil painting or hand-drawn cartoon. This type of cover is very popular in children's fiction. For example, the Harry Potter and Artemis Fowl series use hand-drawn art. Custom illustrated covers can be expensive. You can expect to pay anything from $500 to $1000.

I went down the hand-drawn illustration route as I thought it would suit my book the best. All I had to do now was find an illustrator. There are many freelance covers designers on the market who will be happy to work with you. You can use sites like Fiverr to find a designer, which is one of the cheaper options, or run a design competition with a company like 99designs, as I did with the series logo. In the past, I have used 99designs to run a competition for the cover of a nonfiction book with great results.

This time, however, I looked through my Kindle library at books I liked to find some inspiration. As a big supporter of independent authors, I buy many self-published books. In particular, I had fallen in love with the cover of *Hydra's Wake* by Daniel Jones. On the copyright page, the author credited his cover designer and even included the designer's website. The portfolio page on the website looked fantastic and I was glad to read that the designer creates custom illustrations that he turns into book covers, so I got in touch and sent a brief for the book and what I wanted.

As is quite common with designers and illustrators, I paid fifty percent of the price upfront, and then he started work. The first step was to agree on the concept for the cover. I had a general idea of what I thought would look good, so we discussed it and he produced a rough pencil sketch of the cover image. After a little back and forth, we agreed on the sketch image and he drew and painted the cover.

In just a few days, he had a version of the illustration for me to look at. After a few tweaks, I approved the illustration and he built the cover image.

To create the paperback cover, he needed to know what services would print the book and the page count of the finished book. While I do not cover publishing in this book, I already knew that Amazon KDP and IngramSpark would print the book. IngramSpark would handle the distribution and printing of the paperback in all stores except Amazon, and Amazon would handle the printing of books ordered through their site. I was also going to use a UK print-on-demand company called BookVault to provide copies of the books that I give away for reviews and sell through my website.

Both Amazon and IngramSpark allow you to generate a template file containing the correct book spine measurements to give the designer. As the two services use different paper stock, the books from IngramSpark would be slightly thinner. The books printed through BookVault use the same paper stock as Amazon, so I could reuse that cover.

The designer would produce not only the paperback cover, but also the eBook and audiobook cover, if I decide to make an audiobook. In addition to the templates, I sent him the series log, book blurb and barcode for the back cover. To create the barcode, you need to buy an International Standard Book Number (ISBN). Each country will have a service for buying ISBNs. I bought mine from NielsenISBNStore.com. I had already bought a large batch there a few years ago for my nonfiction work, so I just assigned two of those numbers—one for the paperback and one for the eBook. You can expect to pay anything from $50 to $100 for a single ISBN number, or you can buy a batch of them at a discount.

If you intend to publish only on Amazon, you can let Amazon generate an ISBN for you, but that will prevent you from selling your book anywhere else. I intend to sell my eBook on Amazon, but have my paperback available with any online book retailer, so I needed my own ISBNs. Armed with my ISBN, I went to a website to generate the barcode image. There are many websites that do this, but I used the free barcode generator at Kindlepreneur.com.

The designer now had everything he needed. A few days later, I had approved the final covers and paid the remaining fifty percent of his invoice. The cover was complete, and I was thrilled with it. You can see the final paperback cover below.

Diary of a Martian Paperback cover.

The eBook version consists of the right-hand side of the paperback cover in a separate file, as you can see below.

Diary of a Martian Ebook cover.

Finally, the designer created a cover for an audiobook version of the novel. While I will most likely create an audiobook, I do not expect it to be ready for my initial release, as audiobooks are quite expensive to produce. But the cover looks great.

Diary of a Martian Audiobook cover.

With the book's cover completed, by the beginning of November 2022, I had everything I needed to release *Diary of a Martian*. My plan was to release the novel towards the end of February or early March 2023.

Even though there were several months to wait before the release, I wanted to see what the finished printed book looked like, so I uploaded the cover and print-ready PDF to BookVault and ordered a box of ten books. As they use the same cover and paper stock as Amazon, their books would look identical.

The wait for the printed books was excruciating. The five days felt like forever. Then, one cold Wednesday, the delivery guy turned up with the box.

Final printed copies of Diary of a Martian.

The quality of the printing inside and outside the book looked fantastic, and I was confident that I had created a product that looked as good as anything a traditional publisher would produce.

## On Writing Your First Novel

Interior of the Diary of a Martian paperback.

The final book is presented in the standard 5x8 inch format, so it looks at home next to other novels on the bookshelf. I can't even explain how it feels to open that box from the printers and hold your finished book for the first time. It's almost on a par with a new-born child … just don't say that to my wife.

### Key Takeaway

As much as we don't like to admit it, your book will be judged by its cover, which is why it's important to put resources into having a decent cover designed. There is nothing worse than spending a year or two crafting your perfect book and then falling at the last hurdle with a bad-looking cover that doesn't fit your chosen genre.

You can acquire a good cover by hiring a freelancer directly or through websites like Fiverr or by launching design competitions on websites like 99Designs. When hiring someone, make sure you look through their portfolio of covers and check that they are used to working in your genre. Some designers specialise in specific genres, whereas others are flexible.

I would say that paying for a decent cover designer is just as important as paying for a decent editor. If you can only invest money in two areas of your book's development, then covers and editors are where to focus.

TWENTY-THREE

# Post Implementation Review

When I worked in a corporate environment, whenever we completed a large project, we would hold a post-implementation review (PIR). The purpose of the PIR is to look at the project's lifecycle and work out what went well (so we can do that again next time) and what didn't go well (so we can improve). These meetings were not a witch hunt to apportion blame on anyone; they were genuine fact-finding meetings designed to help teams improve. With that in mind and some corporate blood still flowing through my veins, let's have a look at the making of *Diary of a Martian* and see what I can improve. So, without getting too corporate, let's run the flag up the pole and execute on some blue sky thinking by synergising our synergies (… now I remember why I left).

## What Went Well?

First, I want to look at what went well, as, overall, I feel this project has been a massive success from a creative perspective.

Only time will tell if it's financially successful, but I'm prepared to play a long game.

**Finishing the book**: It goes without saying that completing the book and having it edited, formatted and ready for publication is a tremendous achievement. This project feels very different from my nonfiction books. A novel is much more personal. It's a story that I came up with and developed, so there is a bigger sense of personal achievement. Writing any book is a huge undertaking, and I can safely say that writing a novel is one of the hardest projects I have ever embarked on.

**A well-formed idea to start**: When I first had the idea for *Diary of a Martian*, I wasn't ready to write the novel. I practised my craft with short stories while I developed the novel story further. I had the initial idea in January 2021, but I didn't start writing the first chapter until later in the summer, when I also started the Faber Academy writing course.

By taking my time and not diving into the story straight away, I let the idea mature and I made copious notes. By doing so, I feel that I developed a much stronger story. It was certainly a marathon and not a sprint.

**Acquiring many skills from training**: Taking the Faber Academy course was very valuable. Through it, I gained skills in novel-writing and access to peer reviewers in my class. Peer reviewing each other's chapters helped me immensely. At the end of the course, I received an in-depth analysis of the first 15,000 words of my story from an experienced novelist, which was priceless.

In addition to the Faber course, I watched many online training courses through, for example, Masterclass and LinkedIn Learning. I read writers' craft books. I tried to absorb as much knowledge as I could and found the learning exercise fun. Acquiring new skills and watching myself develop over time was exciting.

Though the first novel is finished, I intend to continue my education so that I can improve with each book that I write.


**Working with a critique partner**: Receiving peer reviews from my Faber Academy classmates was helpful, but it was sometimes too polite, too positive. I didn't want rough treatment, but I did want honest feedback that would help me grow. On this front, hiring an editor to work with as a critique partner was invaluable. Receiving feedback from a professional editor not only helped me shape the book but was also part of my training. I learned a lot.


**Staying on track with a beat sheet**: I have always been a planner for all the book projects I've ever worked on and the novel was no exception. I know full well that if I had tried to write the book by the seat of my pants, I would have veered off track and ended up with an unstructured mess, making the editing process excruciating. I am in awe of pantsers, but that approach is not for me. I crave structure and a plan. That said, I surprised myself a little.

Writing *Diary of a Martian* taught me that I sit between the pantsers and plotters. My beat sheet was detailed enough to keep me on track with the story, but it also gave me the latitude to discover other story elements as I wrote. It offered me the best of both worlds and is the approach I plan to adopt for future novels.

**Quality of the finished book**: One of my goals at the start of this project was to ensure I made a product that looks as good as any book released by a traditional publisher. Self-publishing still has a bit of a stigma for poor quality, which may have been true in previous years. Now, however, high-quality, well-produced independent books can be just as good as their traditionally published cousins. Self-publishing truly is the punk rock of publishing, and I love it.

As I write the final chapter of this book, I'm looking again at that box of printed books sitting on my desk. The cover is colourful and engaging. It fits in with competing books. The book's interior is clean and professional. I can safely say it's the best that I can do. I don't feel as though I have made any compromises that bother me. It's a product that I am proud of.

**Engagement with freelancers**: I have run my own business for many years, which means I have frequently hired freelancers to help me with work that I can't do myself. Most of these interactions have gone very well, but, occasionally, I have hired someone who was difficult to collaborate with or returned poor-quality work.

Thankfully, with *Diary of a Martian*, the people who have helped me have all been very good. From editing and proofreading to graphic design and illustration, everyone has produced work that I am proud of. This also means I already have a team of people to work with for the sequel, so I don't have the stress of trying to find people. I know what they are like to work with and, hopefully, they are comfortable with how I work and what I am trying to achieve.

The success of any creative project is the sum of the people who work on it and I found a great team straightaway.

## What Didn't Go Well?

There are some aspects of producing *Diary of a Martian* that I hope to change for the next book.

**A long time**: It has taken nearly two years from the initial idea of the story to holding a completed book. I stated earlier that it was a good idea to let the idea develop over time while I learned my craft and, while that's okay for the first book, I don't want the sequel to take two years. Now that I have completed one novel and am more comfortable with the process, I would like the production of the next book to be closer to six months or shorter, which I think is possible.

**Expensive**: This first book has cost a lot of money to produce, but I consider that cost an investment in my future work. Investment is very much like controlled gambling and, as with gambling, you should never spend more than you are prepared to lose. I applied that same thought process here. However, if I am going to self-publish my books, I will need to treat publication as a business and try to make that money back over subsequent releases.

In my writing commandments, which I defined at the start of this book and will return to later in this chapter, I stated that I would not prioritise financial gain. That is still true to a degree —the quality of the story and book is the priority. At some point, however, I have to take the financial considerations seriously if novel writing is to be sustainable.

Let's look at the high-level costs of creating this book. Prices are in GBP and are approximations.

> Faber Academy course: £2500
> Editing (including professional critique) and proofreading: £3500
> Logo design: £400
> Cover design and illustration: £700

That's about £7100, which is expensive! I'm including the cost of the Faber Academy course in the production costs, as I used it to help me write book one. The editing and proofreading costs are also high because I paid for two rounds of editing and then final proofreading.

Hiring my editor to act as a critique partner as I wrote the book certainly drove up the costs, but it was a cost I was prepared to pay to help me create a good book. As I said earlier, I wouldn't expect anyone to do that—nor would I recommend it specifically—but it's a decision I made that I feel helped with my education.

Because I run a business that produces content (books and training), and I'm publishing the book through my company, I could justify the costs. If it all goes wrong, I'm lucky enough to be able to lose that money and write off the investment. Going forward, however, the costs for future books will need to come down, and I expect they will—I won't be paying for an expensive training course or the extra round of editing. I also won't need to have a new logo designed. While I think the editing costs I paid (for a single round of editing) are about on par with the industry, the final proofread seemed expensive, and I know I can bring that cost down by using a different freelancer/company. I just wanted the work to be complete, so I went with the same company, but, going forward, I know I can make cost improvements there.

I do have a plan to offset the costs of *Diary of a Martian* and you have that plan before your eyes. I'm experienced in releasing and selling nonfiction books, as well as in carrying out ancillary public speaking and workshops around my books. The production costs for this book were significantly lower than for *Diary of a Martian*, so, hopefully, this book will help me offset the costs in the short term.

It's not unheard of in publishing or any other creative endeavour to produce spin-off products to open up different revenue streams. Cost offsetting wasn't my initial goal with this book; I wrote it because I wanted to and I always like to have a secondary project to work on if I get stuck on the primary project. In the later stages of drafting this manuscript, it occurred to me that this book could help me offset production costs for *Diary of a Martian*. I love it when a plan comes together.

## Personal Writing Commandments

Near the beginning of this book, I defined a series of personal writing commandments I wanted to adhere to. With my corporate background, I like to think strategically and writing these commandments served as a series of guardrails to keep me heading in the right direction.

Let's review those commandments to see how they went and how I feel about them now.

**Thou shalt create a lasting legacy**: While I've had a brilliant career, most of the projects, systems and products that I have contributed to no longer exist or have been superseded, or the companies no longer exist. While working on these projects was a means of earning a living, it bothers me that I don't have a lasting legacy. I'm well aware that this is a classic mid-life crisis symptom, but I wanted to do something about it.

I'm proud of the nonfiction books I have on the market. Yet, as far as a legacy is concerned, being known for self-help or business books isn't very exciting—to my family, at least.

With *Diary of a Martian*, I have a finished novel that I am very proud of and that my family can enjoy, and they have. When my time is up on this planet, I want to be known as Stephen Haunts, the writer of fun fiction, as opposed to Stephen Haunts, the old software developer and corporate trainer.

**Thou shalt create something to pass on to thy children and grandchildren**: Following on from the previous commandment of creating a legacy, I feel I have created something that I can pass on to my children. Both my kids have read *Diary of a Martian* and loved it. They ask questions about the characters, and they discuss the sequel. I feel like I have created something that belongs to them as much as me, and I love that.

The books I wrote about starting businesses or how to communicate with people just don't have the same appeal to my kids. But my fiction does appeal, which feels like a big win to me. No matter what happens when *Diary of a Martian* goes on sale, I have created something that my family and I share and enjoy.

**Thou shalt not prioritise financial gain**: Based on how much it cost me to produce this first book, I can safely say that financial gain wasn't a consideration. It will definitely be a loss leader of a book, as I paid to learn my craft from experienced tutors and for an experienced critique partner.

I also didn't write the book to market. That is, I didn't perform detailed market research on whether this type of book is 'on trend' in the market. That would have been the sensible approach.

I had an idea for a book that I fell in love with and I saw it through to the end. Going forward, as I write the rest of the books in the series, I will need to be more financially conscious and control the costs to bring down production costs, but I won't be doing that at the expense of the idea.

I'm not saying that I won't write to market in the future. Analysing the market is sensible and, as a self-published author, you are in a better position to execute and release at speed on a trend. *Diary of a Martian*, however, is definitely a passion project. And that's okay.


**Thou shalt produce thy best work**: From the beginning, I promised myself I wouldn't compromise on quality to release the book by a certain date and I feel I have achieved that. Sitting here with the finished book on my desk, I don't feel I have compromised on a single aspect of it.

*Diary of a Martian* is the best I can do at this point in time. Of course, in ten years' time, I may look back at the book and say, 'What was I thinking?' I expect every author thinks that. I once read an interview in which J. K. Rowling said that if she were to write the earlier books again, she would do it differently. But, right now, I'm happy that I've done my best work.

When the book hits the market, no matter what other people's feedback is, I know I created the book that I wanted to create and I did it my way. (Have I worked that song into your head yet?)

. . .

**Thou shalt seek to satisfy thy vision above that of anyone else**: The final result of *Diary of a Martian* satisfied my vision. While I drew on extensive feedback and advice from my critique partner, editor and course peers, I made the book I wanted to make—with their help. Whenever I've worked with other companies to produce books or training material, I have always collaborated and worked within someone else's vision or creative framework, which I was happy to do for those projects. However, I consider my fiction writing to be more personal and I'm not willing to compromise.

I think it's safe to say that, the older you get, the more stubborn you become. I certainly have. It's liberating.

**Thou shalt not sacrifice thy rights on the altar of success**: I decided to self-publish instead of entering the chaos of querying for an agent and a traditional publishing deal, partly because I'm not prepared to change my vision to suit someone else's.

I want the freedom to write the books I want to write and release them in a way I see fit. Although fiction is new for me, with my past experience in publishing, I like to think I know what I'm doing and I'd rather succeed or fail by my own actions. I know full well how the odds are stacked against you in modern traditional publishing and I'm not prepared to go through that.

My biggest fear with a traditional publishing deal is losing a book to a state of limbo. If the book is released and is only an average performer for the publisher, they may decide not to do a reprint. Without owning the publishing rights to reissue the book, there would be nothing I could do. I think every writer should be worried about that. Holding onto the rights to my work is one of my overriding guiding principles for my fiction work. It's all about control and I want to be in control.

## What Next?

*Diary of a Martian* was completed at the beginning of November 2022 and this book was completed at the end of December 2022. But I have other projects in the works.

During the summer holidays in 2022, while I was having my enforced break from *Diary of a Martian*, I opened a file in Scrivener and prepared the beat sheet for *Diary of a Martian 2*. By the end of the summer holidays, I had a pretty clear vision for Acts One and Two of that book. The finale in Act Three was a little fuzzy, but I had enough of a plan to make a start. When *Diary of a Martian* had been sent to the proofreader, I began writing Book Two.

My ultimate plan is to release *Diary of a Martian* towards the end of February, or early March 2023. By the time 2023 ends, I hope to have all three books in the Diary of a Martian trilogy written and released. It's a stretch goal and will be challenging, but I like a challenge.

## Thank You

I would like to thank you for reading this book and joining me on my journey to write my first novel. My intention certainly hasn't been to lecture you on the best way to write a novel. Only you can decide your personal approach. If you read this book and agree with my approach, I hope it helps you.

If you read this book and recoiled in horror, all is not lost. You have just learnt how you don't want to write a book, which is just as valuable.

I have a big favour to ask. I released this book myself, through my company, which means I depend on my readers to leave an honest review in the store where they bought the book. I would be grateful if you could leave a review.

I hope you enjoyed this book and gained something from it. Thank you for letting me tell you my story. Now why don't you start writing yours?

## Please Leave a Review

If you enjoyed On Writing Your First Novel, I would be very grateful if you could leave a rating and review at the store you bought the book.

Reviews are very helpful to authors.

# Appendices

# Appendix 1 - Airlock Escape Short Story

The main idea for *Diary of a Martian* came to me in early 2021, when I was experimenting with writing short stories. One of these stories took place in the *Diary of a Martian* universe. What follows is the original short story that helped launch this project.

―――

'Year seven, please settle down,' said Mrs Robertson, standing at the front of the classroom in the civilian block of the New London Martian colony. The civilian block was where everyone in the colony lived. At the centre of the colony was a giant glass dome. Connected to the dome were the different areas where people lived and worked. One of these areas was the school where I was then sitting. It was 9 a.m. on a Monday (NASA Earth Time), and the first lesson was Earth Ancestry, which was my favourite. In this class, we learned about the history and culture of Earth so that we wouldn't lose our connection with our home planet. I am a fourth-generation Martian. I was born on Mars, and I will probably never set foot off of it. Even though I know I will never get off this enormous ball of dust, I am fascinated with Earth. I would love to visit.

'Before we start the lesson, I want to introduce you to a guest from New Beijing,' said Mrs Robertson. New Beijing is a Chinese colony on the northwest side of the Olympus Mons mountain range.

'Everyone, please welcome Mei to the class for this week. Mei, please sit with Elliot,' said Mrs Robertson. Mei walked up to me.

'Pleased to meet you,' she said and smiled at me. Her hazel eyes glimmered with excitement at her field trip.

*Uh oh. A girl is smiling at me. Danger, danger.* 'Hi, erm, pleased to meet you,' I said, raising my arm to shake her hand. *I'm eleven. Who shakes hands at eleven? Put your hand down, you doofus.*

At that moment, my AI assistant, who I named Watson after one of my favourite characters from Sherlock Holmes, spoke through the bio-implanted speaker in my ear.

'Elliot, I am detecting an elevated heart rate and a slight rise in body temperature. Would you like me to run a medical scan and inform the infirmary?'

'No, it's fine,' I whispered awkwardly.

'What was that?' asked Mei.

'Oh, nothing. Just my silly AI asking a question,' I said.

'Who are you calling silly?' said Watson in my ear.

'Not now, Watson.'

Mei smiled. 'My AI does that all the time, although I can't use her until our colony's networks are connected.'

'You don't have your own AI? That must feel weird.'

'It's like leaving a part of me back home.'

'I'll bet. Well, if you need anything, just ask. Welcome to New London,' I said.

'Okay, class. Let's get started. Turn on your screens and select class number five for term two. For the last few weeks, we have been studying the stories of Sherlock Holmes by Arthur Conan Doyle. This week, we are going to look at the twenty-first-century classic Harry Potter,' said Mrs Robertson. 'Harry Potter is a fantasy adventure about a boy who finds out he is a wizard and goes to study at a mythical school called Hogwar...' Mrs Robertson was interrupted by the dull thud of an explosion. The classroom shook.

Just as Mrs Robertson was about to speak, the red lights came on and an announcement came over the speakers. 'Structural compromise detected. Please evacuate immediately. Please evacuate. This is not a drill.'

---

'Okay, class. Leave everything behind and form a line, just as we practiced. Elliot, please stay with our guest at all times. Nobody panic. We have practiced this many times.'

'Elliot, what's going on?' asked Mei.

'It's the evacuation alarm. We usually know in advance if there is going to be a drill, so this sounds real.' Mei didn't have to say anything. Her eyes pierced my soul. She was scared and away from home.

'Stay with me. I'll show you what to do. I promise.'

I got up, moved toward my place in line and gestured for Mei to come with me.

'Stay behind me.'

'I will,' said Mei.

When the entire class had lined up, Mrs Robertson led us all out of the classroom and down the corridor. The corridor's usual grey walls were bathed in red emergency lighting. Lighting strips on the ground guided us to the nearest airlock. Every building in the colony has enough airlock space and space suits to enable a mass evacuation.

Mrs Robertson stood in front of the door to our class's designated airlock. Her iris was scanned and the door opened. She counted us as we moved into the room. 'Everyone, get your suits on quickly, but stay calm.'

'Life support compromised! Please evacuate immediately,' came an announcement over the address system, increasing everyone's sense of urgency.

'Elliot, these suits look different from ours. What do I do?' said Mei.

'I'll help you. These suits are one-size-fits-all for children.'

I pulled out two suits from the rack for me and Mei.

'Put your feet in the boots like me, and then put the suit on like a big coat.' Mei copied me and put it on.

'It's far too big.'

'Pull the front of the suit together and then press the button on your left arm that says "compress".'

Mei pressed the button, and the suit snapped shut and shrank down to her size, the suit going tight as the oxygen escaped it. It was like she was being shrink-wrapped. I did the same.

'Okay, now press the lock button. The suit will be sealed.'

I took a helmet and turned around to Mei.

'Going to put this on your head now. Ready?'

'Yes, ready.'

I placed the helmet over Mei's head and turned it until I felt the click of the latch and then did the same with my helmet. I checked the badge on Mei's left arm, which had the number forty-three on it.

'Watson, patch comms into suit forty-three,' I commanded my AI assistant.

'Communications routed,' said Watson.

'Mei, can you hear me?'

'Yes, I can hear you.'

'On your head-up display, can you see the oxygen level?'

'Yes, it says one hundred.'

'Good, your tank is full. What about pressure? Underneath the oxygen level, what does that say?'

'That also says one hundred.'

'Okay, you are ready. Good to go.'

Our comms links suddenly crackled, and Mrs Robertson spoke.

'Class, this is not a drill. I don't know what has happened, but the building is about to lose structural integrity, and life support has been compromised. We will likely have to leave the building and walk on the surface.'

Everyone in the class exchanged glances. You could feel the fear in the room.

'There is a powerful dust storm outside, so listen carefully. I will add each of you to a tether cable. Please form a line immediately,' said Mrs Robertson, with a sense of urgency in her voice.

'Do you want to go in front of or behind me, Mei?'

'Behind, I'll let you lead,' said Mei.

'No problem.'

Mrs Robertson started making her way down the line and attached the tethering cable to each of our belts.

'Have you ever walked on the surface before?' Mei asked.

'No, we don't do our first surface walk until we're twelve. I'm a few months away.'

'We start at eleven. I did my first walk a few weeks ago,' said Mei.

'You're more qualified than me,' I said, trying to force a smile.

'Structural integrity failure imminent. Three minutes to life-support failure,' noted the colony computer.

'I wish I were home,' said Mei.

I couldn't blame her. She had only been in our colony for a few hours. I took Mei's gloved hand and squeezed tight.

'You will be fine. I'll help you though this.'

'Thank you, Elliot,' said Mei as she smiled at me again, although this smile was not as sweet as the one earlier in the morning.

'Class, listen carefully,' said Mrs Robertson. 'In a moment, a personnel carrier will pull up outside, and a member of the colony security services will meet us. I will drop the air pressure in this airlock and open the outside door, and we will walk about ten meters. That's the closest the carrier can get. They can't reverse in because the storm could damage the carrier.' As she said this, she walked down the line of children, double-checking the tethers and the suits' pressure and oxygen levels.

'The tether will be connected to a winch in the personnel carrier and you will slowly be pulled out. Once you are in the carrier, the security service members will disconnect you from the tether. You are to find a seat immediately and engage the seat lock,' said Mrs Robertson. Everyone nodded their compliance.

'The sandstorm is fierce; it will try to knock you off your feet. Everyone, take your right hand and put it on the shoulder of the person in front of you. You are all responsible for trying to keep the person in front of you stable until you are in the carrier. Do you understand?'

'Yes, Mrs Robertson,' everyone said together.

'Watson, do you know has happened?' I asked my AI assistant.

'Negative. There is a communication blackout. I cannot access the logs to determine the cause. All I know is that there has been a sudden depressurisation in the main colony complex,' said Watson.

I could see out the window of the airlock. A personnel

carrier pulled up, and a man in a spacesuit struggled to walk up to the door, blown sideways by wind and dust. He grabbed onto a handle outside the airlock door.

'Okay, class. Emergency depressurisation in five... four... three... two... one...,' said Mrs Robertson, who sounded like she was trying to suppress the sound of panic in her voice. She lifted the flap covering the control panel on the wall and then pushed in a large red dial and twisted it to the left. A button lit up in green, and she pressed it.

Suddenly, all the air was removed from the room. Everyone jolted forward under the force of the rapid depressurisation. The lights dimmed as a piercingly loud alarm sounded. As the pressure dropped to the same level as that of the Martian surface, the sound of the alarm grew quieter. All I could hear was my and Mei's breathing, because I still had my comms patched into her helmet.

'Class, I am about to open the door. Everyone put your right hand on the shoulder of the person in front of you,' said Mrs Robertson.

She pulled out the big handle on the airlock door, rotated it clockwise once and pushed the handle in. As she did so, the whole door moved forward and then to the side. We were exposed to the Martian atmosphere. With the dust storm raging, I could immediately feel the atmospheric pressure. It felt like a sucking sensation that pulled me towards the door. I pulled back on the person in front of me and could feel Mei doing the same to me as everyone tried to stabilise their tether partner.

A member of the security team walked into the airlock, took the end of the tether line and turned to struggle back to the personnel carrier. If he were struggling, what chance would we have as children? I turned around and could see Mrs Robertson attach herself to the end of the tether. The teacher would be the last to leave so that they would leave no children behind.

The line started to move as the first of my classmates left the airlock and began the short walk to the personnel carrier. The force of the dust storm nearly knocked him off his feet, but the security officer grabbed him and helped him into the carrier. The entire line quickly processed out onto the Martian surface.

'Are you ready, Mei?'

'I am, Elliot.'

'Okay, about to leave the airlock. Hold on tight.'

'I've got you,' said Mei, and I could feel the grip of her glove on my shoulder get tighter.

---

I stepped out of the airlock with Mei close behind me. The force of the storm nearly knocked me off my feet. With each footstep, I felt as though someone was trying to push me over. The tether felt tight as the winch pulled us towards the carrier. Suddenly, I felt a pain on my side; a piece of debris hit me, and I fell to the ground. An alarm started to sound in my helmet, and my oxygen levels began to drop.

'Elliot!'

Mei tried grabbing me to lift me up, but she was struggling to stay upright herself. A security officer ran over and lifted me up. I pointed to the oxygen monitor on my arm.

'Control, one child has an oxygen leak. I am disconnecting him from the tether and bringing him in immediately,' said the officer. He unclipped me from the cable, hoisted me up and started running with me to the carrier, fighting against the wind with each footstep. As we entered the carrier, another security officer grabbed me, lifted me and, in one move, pushed me into a seat, where I was immediately locked into place. He pulled an oxygen feed tube down from the panel above my head and connected it to the reserve oxygen port on my back. As he did, my nearly empty oxygen tank disengaged, and I started breathing through the carrier's supply. The security officer gave me a thumbs-up, and I returned the gesture. That was scary.

It wasn't long before Mei sat next to me and was secured in her seat. I could hear her heavy breathing over the comms link.

'Are you okay, Elliot?'

'Yeah, I didn't see what hit me, but it damaged the oxygen line on my suit. I was leaking air quickly.'

'It looked like some junk from outside the colony blew towards you,' Mei said.

'I'm okay. I will have a bruise, but nothing bad.'

As I finished speaking, I saw Mrs Robertson climb on board the carrier, and the doors closed behind her. She started making her way down the seats, counting everyone. When she had finished, she turned to the driver and gave a thumbs-up before sitting down and locking herself into her seat.

'Class, well done for a calm and orderly evacuation. We are going to be driven to the nearest building with a pressurised cargo bay. It's the closest one with a cargo bay we can enter without having to take another walk in the storm. It will take about ten minutes. Keep your helmets locked and an eye on your oxygen levels.'

Once Mrs Robertson had finished talking to the class, she patched directly through to me.

'How are you, Elliot? Are you hurt?'

'No, I'm okay. I had an oxygen leak. I am breathing on the carrier supply,' I said back to her.

'Good to hear you are okay, Elliot. Monitor your oxygen levels and suit pressure.'

'Mrs Robertson, what building are we going to?'

'Terraforming Building Two.'

'Terraforming Two, good. That's where my dad works.'

'You'll be back with him soon, Elliot.'

I turned my head to look out of the window. All I could see was a sea of red dust being blown at the window. You could usually see a spectacular mountain range here, but not today. We picked a great time to evacuate—during a *storm*. Dust storms are a common occurrence on Mars and can last for weeks at a time, and this storm was quite heavy.

---

After a short drive, we approached Terraforming Building Two. The large cargo bay doors opened, and we drove in with two other personnel carriers. The doors closed.

'Pressurising cargo bay. Please stand by,' rang out an announcement over the bay speakers and in our helmets. As the room filled with oxygen, I could feel the pressure changing in my suit. 'Cargo bay pressure normal,' came over the speakers, and the lights went from red to normal.

'Class, you can remove your helmets,' said Mrs Robertson over the radio. I entered the unlock code into the keypad on my arm, which sounded a short sound burst in my helmet. I twisted the helmet off and took a deep breath.

'Here, let me help you, Mei.'

'Thank you, Elliot.'

I repeated the unlock procedure and helped remove Mei's helmet. I could see the relief in her eyes because we were in the safety of another building.

Mrs Robertson unclipped the oxygen line from the carrier that was connected to my life-support backpack and patted me on the shoulder several times. She didn't need to say anything. I could tell she was relieved to be in another building with working life support.

'How are you, Mei?' asked Mrs Robertson.

'I'm okay. Elliot helped me with the suit.'

'Glad to hear it,' said Mrs Robertson and smiled. 'Okay, children, you can all leave the carrier. Please stay together.'

I got up and walked along with Mei and the rest of my class. A security marshal directed us over to one corner of the cargo bay. I looked up and saw my dad standing there, looking around with a panicked expression on his face. As soon as he saw me, he ran over.

'Elliot, I am so happy you are okay,' Dad said as he gave me a big hug.

'I'm fine, Dad. I got hit by some debris trying to get to the carrier, which ruptured my oxygen line, but I'm fine.'

'This whole situation has caught everyone off guard,' said Dad.

As he said this, he spotted my new friend.

'Hello, you must be Mei,' he said.

'How do you know who I am?' said Mei.

'I have been working with your mum for a while now. She is my counterpart in terraforming work over in New Beijing.'

'I wish I could speak to her,' said Mei.

'All our communications are disabled,' I said. 'I couldn't even contact you.'

'All civilian communications are disabled as a security measure. Luckily, though, people in my position still have communications enabled, as they're needed to keep the life support systems working. I can call your mum, Mei.'

'Can you? Thank you. I would be so grateful,' said Mei, her face beaming.

'Sam, start call to Shu at Terraforming Station Nine,' said Dad to his AI assistant. After a few seconds, it connected him to Mei's mum through his earpiece.

'Shu, this is David. Mei is safe. We evacuated the school to our terraforming station. She wants to talk to you.'

Dad pulled out his portable communicator device.

'Sam, transfer the call to my handset.'

He handed Mei the communicator.

Mei walked away to talk to her mum in private.

'Dad, what's happened?' I asked. 'We heard what sounded like an explosion and the classroom shook before we had to evacuate.'

'It looks like someone tried to destroy the entrance to the new hyper-loop tunnel connecting us to New Beijing,' said Dad with a worried look on his face.

'Why would someone do that?'

'Not everyone is so happy that we've joined our colony with the Chinese. Someone wants us to remain a separate colony,' said Dad.

'But why? We're all trying to achieve the same goal of a second home away from Earth.'

'I know. It makes little sense and we don't yet know who set the bomb off, so we are still at risk.'

'This is the sort of issue countries on Earth used to fight over. We should know better than that now,' I said. I studied Earth's history in my Ancestry class and how countries used to fight over natural resources, each thinking their country's needs were more important than those of other countries.

In the space of a day, I feel as if we have gone from a peaceful colony trying to terraform a new world to repeating the same mistakes made by our ancestors on Earth. I don't know what the future will hold, but, after today, Mars feels like a more dangerous world.

# Appendix 2 - Dealing with Criticism

Many years ago, I wrote the following blog post about dealing with criticism of your work in the workplace. While this post isn't specific to writing, I hope you find it helpful when sharing your work. When you write a novel, you can expect criticism from lots of different people: editors and proof-readers, family, friends and, once you release your work, your readers. Criticism can sting when it's not positive, but I hope the following blog post will help you deal with the comments.

---

For many people, being offered criticism isn't always pleasurable or appreciated, no matter if it's from a family member, good friend or a work colleague. Whether it's taken as constructive or causes personal turmoil, criticism can be quite difficult to receive and process. The result may be helpful if that was the intention, or it can be one of those difficult things to accept and forget.

Being criticised at work has been known to have a significant positive or negative impact on employee morale and, in turn, productivity. Whether the criticism is handed out verbally, by email, through direct messaging systems or even over a social media platform, more often than not, the one given the task of providing feedback often fails to consider how the content might be received, especially when it's unfavourable.

The goal of criticism is usually to improve results at work, without considering the connection between morale and productivity.

Some research has shown that criticism of any kind actually closes down the same brain centres that are otherwise activated when talking about positive things. So, it's simple to understand how being criticised by a manager or colleague might evoke negative thoughts, embarrassment and humiliation. When a group of employees are put on the defensive and feel dejected from negative performance reviews, it can be devastating to a company's bottom line.

Receiving criticism at work, whether it's called 'feedback', 'performance reviews' or 'advice', likely won't go away. As a cornerstone of corporate culture, more often than not, criticism is how companies get things done. So, if your chances of avoiding criticism at work are slim, it's in your best interest, as giver or receiver, to understand what criticism is and how best to harness its capacity to create productive output and positive people.

## Types of Criticisers

There are libraries full of psychology texts filled with numerous chapters dedicated to the breakdown and classification of the different species of human criticisers. The same can be said about how the different types of criticism might be grouped.

**Three Types of Criticism?**

For example, one former psychologist concluded there are three different kinds of criticism: friendly, objective and hostile. A friendly critique comes from a place of caring and is aimed at helping the person. An objective criticism, as the name suggests, is backed by facts and research only. The person has no status or influence. Hostile criticism is inherently negative. Its target is the person and the person's ideas, and it is meant to destroy.

**Four Types of Criticisers**

While the above-mentioned three types of criticism make sense philosophically or theoretically, when you're at work, it's your co-workers, managers and others giving and receiving criticism. Thus, the more sensible approach to understanding workplace criticism is a concept cleverly devised by journalist Ann Friedman that suggests there are four types of criticisers in our midst. Do any of these sound familiar?

**Critics:** Critics might as well be robots. They are smart people and may actually be considered experts in your field. At work, the critic may be your department manager or a colleague with more seniority or experience than you. Critics are focused on your work performance or, according to them, how and why you're doing it wrong. They're not interested in you as the swell person you say you are.

**Haters:** Haters criticise because they can and because they're hoping it elicits your reaction—ideally for them, you feel some version of bad. You know what's worse? They don't care how bad you feel; they're uninterested in your growth and betterment. They barely know you, if at all. So, it's all the more puzzling why they have this irrational desire to put you down.

**Frenemies:** 'A wolf in sheep's clothing' might come to mind when describing frenemies. A word mashup of 'friend' and 'enemy', these criticisers can be a little tricky to spot at first, because you definitely know each other. At work, your frenemy is a colleague who made you believe they had your back, but as soon as an opportunity opened up, they were right there to put you down. To add insult to injury, your frenemy's criticism has nothing to do with improving your work performance and everything to do with you as a person.

**Lovers:** Lovers (in the most platonic sense of the word) want you to succeed. They put the time, effort and excitement into your personal growth and improvement. There is nothing irrational about their criticism. In fact, it's downright constructive. Working with and for lovers will get you far because that's how they live.

## Dealing with Criticism

Reacting to criticism, regardless of its origin or intent, is as common as anything we do as humans. For many of us, it's practically automatic. In the heat of the moment, we'll let our emotions take over and end up regretting it several hours later—and that's just from feedback you knew you were getting. Imagine how things would develop if you were offered unsolicited advice or surprise feedback from a critic or lover.

If you're prone to reaction, you are unlikely to hear what's being said about you or your work. Why get angry? What do you have to gain by putting up walls and ignoring feedback? Instead of getting defensive, you might consider that constructive criticism can be a blessing in disguise. The benefits far outnumber any drawbacks to being on the receiving end of constructive feedback.

Why not learn to be less defensive and more logical about how to handle criticism in a more dignified and progressive way? Below are six ways to handle the awkward encounter with grace and tact.

## Keep an Open Mind and Listen

Do not react. Instead, try actively listening to what's being said about you or your work. This is no place for pride, so lock it away for the day. Take copious notes and assume that the intentions of the person providing the feedback are genuine and that they've truly got your back and want you to succeed.

**Know Your Triggers:** Easier said than done. This isn't just a sibling who knows which of your buttons to push to get you angry. This is your job. The criticiser probably doesn't want to harm you. Take an objective point of view and try to identify exactly what was said to make you feel defensive or upset. You probably already know the answer; you've just never had to articulate it before. For example, if your manager suggests ways for you to improve your presentation skills, see that as your chance to become better at something, as opposed to taking it as an insult.

**Think First, Respond Later:** Check your temper at the door. It won't help you in most work situations. More often than not, stalling your reaction, no matter how difficult it is for you, is the best way to get a handle on your situation. Take some time first to digest the full story. If you must, wait until you get home to get angry and then say everything you *really* wanted to say earlier. Use an understanding friend or family member as a stand-in for your criticiser.

**Use It to Become Better:** Once you've blown off the steam you generated from recent criticism, come back to the table and understand how to use that criticism to become better at what you do. Hopefully, that's what your criticiser was intending on doing—helping you become better. Can you imagine going through life without someone giving you feedback? Don't just bury your head in the sand. If there's something valuable you can learn from, go for it!

**Go Easy on Yourself:** Getting criticised isn't the end of the world. Keep in mind that we all have something to learn and the more we know, the better. Making mistakes or actually failing to do something perfectly does not make you a failure. It means you're working and making progress. So, take it easy on yourself.

**Express Gratitude:** Say thank you for your constructive criticism, even when it feels hard to digest. Your positive attitude may come as a shock to your criticiser. Responding with gratitude will turn the tables on your criticisers—even more so if they were frenemies or haters. Besides, it's always better to take the high road, no matter what type of critique was thrown at you.

## Dealing with Criticisers

It can be a challenge knowing what to do with criticism when it's coming from any of the different types of criticisers. Unless you really know them on a personal or professional level, your approach should always be rational and level-headed. More often than not, the source of the criticism is just as important as the content of the critique. Here's how you can deal with the critics, haters, frenemies and lovers in your life.

**Dealing with Critics:** Pay keen attention to critics. They aren't being negative for the sake of being negative. Since they don't know you personally, as frenemies do, their criticism is unbiased and usually quite constructive. Take what they've imparted to you and work on the areas they've pointed out that need improvement.

**Dealing with Haters:** For haters, the best reaction is no reaction. Criticising is what they love doing. Nothing they say is meant to be helpful, so do your best version of one person actively ignoring another. Their 'feedback' is counterproductive. Just know that some people will always have something negative to say about you—especially if you've become successful.

**Dealing with Frenemies:** Accept their words gracefully, but don't take them personally. Better yet, use this as an opportunity to re-evaluate your relationship with them. Now you know what you can and can't say to your frenemy, because, if they can, they will use it against you. On the off chance that they're not making it personal, try to determine if they're criticising your work or your work style. If it's the latter, ignore it. If it's the former, fix it.

**Dealing with Lovers:** Because they are wholly invested in you, their criticism is more akin to friendly feedback in support of your growth and happiness. You can definitely seek their advice on what they believe requires work and how to approach these changes. You have to tell lovers to just say what's on their mind, because they're more concerned with sparing your feelings than telling you what you need to hear. Appeal to their sense of the greater good by letting them know that their feedback will help you become better at what you do.

## Conclusion

If you make any form of content that you put out into the world, criticism will always follow. In my experience, a lot of feedback tends to be positive. Sometimes, I get constructive criticism from someone who genuinely cares and wants to help. I always appreciate that. From time to time, I also get people just being nasty jerks, especially on Twitter, which seems to be where the dregs of society lurk among some genuinely nice people. If I am honest, people giving bad and ugly feedback used to hurt. After all, I am human and have feelings. Over time, I have learned just to ignore feedback that isn't helpful.

My dad had a phrase he always used, which I think about often: 'Opinions are like arseholes. Everyone has one. Most of them stink.' I think this is wise advice.

In my opinion, if you create anything, be it a blog post, video or report for work, do your best work and unleash it to the world only when you are happy with it. Provided you are satisfied with the end result, nobody else's opinion should matter. If someone wants to give praise or useful constructive feedback, that's fantastic. If someone wants to be a jerk to you, just ignore them; they are not worth the effort. Go forth and create your best work and enjoy the process.

# Appendix 3 - How to Give Constructive Criticism

I wrote the following blog post many years ago about giving constructive criticism in the workplace. While this isn't about writing specifically, I hope you find it helpful. As a writer you may be asked to give a critique on a fellow writer's work. You could be giving a critique of a short piece of writing or an entire book as a beta-reader. Either way, this blog post will help you give good quality, constructive criticism.

---

Nearly 16,000 managers were surveyed in two separate studies by the leadership development consultancies Zenger and Folkman, respectively. It might come as a shock to you that 44% of the managers responded that they find the act of giving feedback stressful, especially when it is negative. One-fifth of the managers avoid it entirely, which raises a question: If our employees aren't giving 100% to their work, can we, as managers, be at fault? Imagine dealing with an unproductive, unpunctual and irresponsible employee on your team who hasn't been told about these traits yet. Picture them coming to you and asking for a raise. Shocking as it may seem, you are the one at fault for never pointing out the worst.

Criticism, like evaluations, is an important aspect of being a manager. As managers, it is imperative that we understand the importance of giving and receiving feedback. Feedback, especially constructive feedback, is a respectful way of helping employees better themselves. It is a means of guiding them with honesty, directness and dignity, while not damaging their feelings and ego. When delivered in the right manner, it doesn't create uneasy spaces within the four walls of the office but rather strengthens interpersonal bonds, which ultimately boosts employees' productivity and efficiency.

Most managers find it hard to offer constructive criticism when it comes to pointing out areas of improvement. They struggle with finding the right balance between advising and criticising, fear their words might hurt the feelings of their employees, worry if criticism will negatively impact their employees' productivity by demoralising them and so forth.

But here's a fact—you are going to have to get comfortable delivering constructive criticism. Really, really, really comfortable! Although it is hard enough to deliver it to anyone, it is the hardest to deliver to someone who always gets on your nerves or underperforms. To say the least, such situations require mastering the art of giving constructive criticism.

Therefore, this article explores how to give constructive criticism in a way that doesn't hurt the receiver's feelings, the differences between constructive and non-constructive criticism and how to use empathy to improve the impact of the criticism.

## Understanding the Difference Between Constructive and Non-Constructive Criticism

The primary concern with giving constructive criticism lies in knowing what it is and, more importantly, what it is not. Confused? Let us put it more directly. Not all the feedback you give is constructive in nature. Sometimes, your words, expressions and actions can say something completely different from what you believe they are saying. You might think you are just advising someone to improve, but they might take offence to the language, expressions or actions used. Faulting someone without the use of appropriate language and actions can seem disrespectful and aggressive—thus, it comes out as non-constructive criticism.

Not all criticism is constructive. It can sometimes be difficult to tell the difference between constructive and non-constructive criticism, whether you're giving or receiving it. So, what really is constructive and non-constructive or destructive criticism, and how do we differentiate between the two?

Constructive criticism is the practice of instilling confidence in the employee by gracefully and tactfully pointing out the areas that need improvement so that they can develop professionally on the job. Think of it as an art teacher evaluating the work of one of their students and telling the student that although the art is brilliant as it is, there is still room for improvement. The ultimate goal is to encourage the student without putting them down or making them feel unvalued or bad. When feedback is perceived in this manner, the receiver doesn't feel like a complete failure and stays focused on betterment. The receiver feels like they are on the right track and just needs to put in more effort to become a master.

Conversely, non-constructive feedback or criticism aims at belittling the employee and insulting them outright. It is a practice used to put down someone and hurt their feelings. Instead of telling the employee that they are good as they are and just need to work on some areas of their work, a manager who criticises destructively would say something like, 'That was one terrible performance. I am so ashamed of you. I should have chosen someone else to do it. This was a total waste of time.' Now, if you notice, this type of feedback lacks two things. First, it labels the employee a complete failure without any positive acknowledgement and, second, it doesn't emphasise the areas where the employee needs to improve. The employee just knows that they have made a complete fool of themselves but not how to rectify it. What is the end result? An employee leaving the room feeling defeated without knowing how they could have improved their work.

To further differentiate between constructive and non-constructive criticism, here are the key differences to take note of and self-assess on. What have you been labelling as constructive criticism? Do you need to update your approach?

In constructive criticism, the focus is on the present situation. The feedback given is only for something presented or done at the moment. When opting to critique someone constructively, ensure that the feedback relates to just one situation. That way, the receiver won't feel like they are being critiqued for being a failure as an employee but rather for something specific they did poorly. Constructive feedback isn't offered for something done in the past. Otherwise, it isn't constructive.

Destructive or non-constructive feedback often focuses on past errors. It usually implies that the person is not fit for any task whatsoever and is thus demeaning. It sounds something like, 'Are you going to repeat the same blunder again?' or 'I hope this is better than the last report you sent me.' Such statements are condescending to the receiver and make them feel devalued and disrespected. Why? Because they might have worked extremely hard this time, putting their very soul into their work and your attitude and words can really hurt them.

The language used in constructive feedback isn't judgemental. The receiver shouldn't feel as if they are being judged or objectified. Therefore, the use of objective language is crucial when giving constructive feedback. You should only state the facts or things observed. The employee shouldn't feel evaluated negatively on something personal.

Non-constructive feedback is usually accompanied by personal insults and invectives. It is more about the personality of the individual and less about their performance faults. An example of this would look something like, 'You are clearly clueless about what was asked of you. I am highly disappointed with what you have put forward. I guess it isn't in you.'

This is a clear affront, and this kind of feedback is highly demotivating. Instead, be objective and only pinpoint the mistakes rather than attacking an employee's work ethic.

Constructive feedback is usually specific. It addresses the fault without beating about the bush. It is a direct and straightforward way of telling the employee where they were lacking and, thus, where they need to improve. At the end of it, the receiver walks out knowing exactly what they need to work on and what actions will help them improve.

Non-constructive criticism is usually vague. It isn't aimed directly at the problem. As a consequence, it leaves the receiver confused. This confusion happens when managers feel shy or cautious about speaking their views out loud. Therefore, they expect the receiver to take note and rectify the concerns on their own. However, this can further exacerbate the problem, as both the giver and receiver might end up on completely different pages. Therefore, when giving feedback constructively, try to directly highlight points that need to be addressed and upgraded. The more candid you are, the higher the chances of improvement.

Now that you are familiar with the distinctions between constructive and non-constructive criticism, the next step is to learn how to critique constructively.

### Managers Take Note: Giving Constructive Criticism

No one likes to be criticised, no matter who the critic is. This is one reason why it is important to master the art of critiquing. As a manager or supervisor, chances are you will come across several situations where your word and observation about employee performances will be in question. So how do you go about critiquing someone constructively?

Here are some unspoken rules to abide by to ensure that by the time you are done giving your feedback, your employee's face doesn't reflect defeat or exasperation.

**Do It One-on-One**: The first unsaid rule is to never publicise. Even public praise can leave awkward silences; criticism is a different story altogether. Whenever you find yourself in such a situation where feedback is required, summon the receiver for a one-on-one meeting. Not everyone likes to be the centre of attention. A one-on-one meeting will feel more comfortable for both you and your employee. Besides, this isn't a parade but personal feedback and, thus, should be provided in a calm and comfortable setting.

**Choose the Right Time**: Time and place matters. If you sense that the employee is already down or frazzled about their performance, there is no need to further embarrass them then and there. Your feedback can wait a day or two when they are in the right frame of mind and seem motivated to improve.

**Take It Slow**: It is best not to blurt everything out in one outburst. Remember, your goal is to help your employees overcome their shortcomings and not lose all their remaining self-confidence. Too much feedback given at one time can intimidate the employee. Pick one or two issues to talk about at most, and leave the rest for another time and another day.

**Sandwich It!** If you have been providing constructive criticism (even when doing it wrong), you might have come across the sandwich method once or twice. This is a popular technique for offering constructive feedback without hurting employees' feelings. This eliminates the guilt and embarrassment that an employee might feel when called out for their mistakes. Here's how you can use it to structure your feedback appropriately.

Start on a positive note by talking about the good things that the employee does/did. Then, slide in the parts that can be improved. Finally, end on a hopeful and positive note. This doesn't demean the receiver, they don't lose their confidence in themselves and they are better able to apply your comments towards self-improvement.

**Be a Good Listener**: The communication between the critic and the receiver should be two-way. You must also listen to your employee's reasons for the particular blunder, especially if it has occurred repeatedly. Ask probing questions about why the employee behaves or acts in a certain way. Try to understand their point of view, hear out their concerns and then advise accordingly. Seek suggestions on what they think would be the best solution to overcome the issue. Discuss whether training or counselling is required.

**Offer Clarity**: Explain what went wrong. Avoid suggesting dual meanings or conveying complex messages. If there is something that your employee needs to work on, let them know that clearly. Offering clarity should be the ultimate goal of any form of feedback so that it is understood by the receiver. Mixed messages, especially the ones with a 'but' in between them, can be confusing. For instance, starting a sentence with praise and then using 'but' before coming to the actual point can create a contradiction. The employee will have a nanosecond to wipe that expression of pride from their face as you finish the sentence. When you link praises and faults with words like 'but', 'however' or 'although', the receiver hears: 'Don't believe a word of what I just said before. Here's how you messed up!'

**Be Empathic**: Express your concern so that the employee doesn't feel demeaned. Show them that the reason you are highlighting these issues is so you can help them improve and that you really wish to see them improve. A tone of concern, paired with the right gestures and words, adds a certain amount of sincerity. Ensure that the content of the feedback isn't lost in sarcasm, anger, disappointment or frustration. Be considerate and let them know that you care.

**Avoid Pointing Fingers**: Focus on the situation, issue or behaviour. Criticise the work, rather than the individual. Focus on the observable facts and state them gracefully, without making the employee feel under scrutiny. Explain your point of view instead of just pointing out faults. Don't state things like, 'You are always late. Why can't you be punctual?' Instead, say something like, 'When you are late, everyone worries. It delays our rehearsals, and the event starts late. Please try to be on time so that everything runs smoothly, as we planned.'

Even though this is criticism, it isn't blunt or degrading. It is purely stating the facts using appropriate words that don't come across as bossy.

**End with Words of Encouragement**: Avoid going over past mistakes as your closing statement. Check that the employee has received the feedback without feeling defensive or disheartened. If there is something that needs fixing, ensure that it is talked about in detail at the start or middle of the conversation. Ending on a negative note will leave the employee demotivated, and all the stage-setting will be of no use. Chances are, they will only remember the discouraging words and forget everything else. It is like telling someone, 'Thank you for coming, but I wished you hadn't!'

## How Empathy Improves Employee Reactions to Constructive Criticism

Feedback coming from someone dear is always welcomed and appreciated. In fact, criticism can be the best gift for someone you love. However, since workplaces require a more professional and controlled attitude, there can be little room for relational investment. This is one reason why criticism, be it positive or negative, is often received as an insult.

But this practice can and should be revised. Empathy should be a primary tool to use when critiquing someone's work. Time and again, it has proven effective. Employees respond to constructive criticism better when they feel that their manager or boss is a well-wisher and really wants to see them improve and prosper. Empathic concern kickstarts positive changes and ripples throughout the firm.

To give feedback with empathy, it is important that you, as a manager, are emotionally intelligent. When done right, feedback can result in drastic changes in the efficiency, productivity and overall state of mind of your employees. It will inspire instead of degrade them, motivate instead of discourage them and foster trust instead of threats. A lack of empathy on the manager's part can create dissonance. Organisations where feedback is given in a degrading manner and without empathy can never flourish, as the employees will never feel motivated and inspired to work their best.

The impact of empathic concerns when giving negative feedback was illustrated powerfully in a study of 177 people who participated through an online marketplace, Amazon's Mechanical Turk. During the study, a video-based scenario was presented. In the first half of the experiment, all the participants were shown a video of a manager giving negative criticism to his employees. In the second part of the experiment, half of the participants were shown the same manager now demonstrating empathic concern, while the other half watched the manager continue giving feedback without empathy.

The participants were then asked for their views on the manager's performance. The findings suggested that leaders who showed empathic concern while giving feedback were perceived as good bosses. Their style was rated more highly and as more effective in terms of helping employees improve. It was also revealed that when leaders showed empathic concern, the emotional reactions of the employees were less demotivated and more hopeful. The leader who showed empathic concern in the video was also viewed as more promotable.

The bottom line is that your most direct path to success as a team leader comes through clear, caring constructive criticism. It's simply worth the time and effort to address your employees' faults in supportive and positive ways!

# Diary of a Martian Extract

In this book, I have talked a lot about the creation of my debut middle-grade science fiction novel, *Diary of a Martian*. The book has been a labour of love for me. What follows is the prologue and first four chapters from the Novel.

If you like what you read, then the final book is available as a paperback, and ebook. You can read more about the book and find purchasing links at https://www.stephenhauntsfiction.com, or by scanning the following QR Code.

# Prologue

Earth Date: 9th January 2154

**Mars Orbital Space Station (MOSS)**

*[Reconstructed from declassified camera footage, systems logs and reports.]*

"Shuttle Archimedes, you're cleared to dock at hangar seventeen." Lieutenant Sarah Taylor's voice came through the comms system in the control centre of the Mars Orbital Space Station (MOSS), floating high above the Martian surface.

"Affirmative, engaging autopilot and beginning docking procedure," replied Captain Ramirez.

"Autopilot confirmed. We're bringing you in." Sarah watched the shuttle dock from her command console.

"Sarah, now the formalities are over, come and meet me when we've docked. I have that package for your son," said Captain Ramirez.

"Thank you, Sam. Elliot will be thrilled."

The Archimedes turned around on its final approach, ready to reverse into the docking clamps. Guidance rockets puffed small jets of gas to keep the shuttle on target. The gap between the shuttle and space station shrank until the docking clamps snapped shut, locking the shuttle in place. Captain Ramirez knew what he was doing. This was his sixth time docking at MOSS.

"Docking procedure complete. The hangar bay is now pressurised, ready to unload your cargo. Welcome back to MOSS, Captain Ramirez," said Lieutenant Taylor.

"Affirmative. Starting shuttle unloading. It's good to be back."

Sarah turned to her colleagues in shuttle control. "Permission to supervise the Archimedes's unload."

Captain Ronson looked up. "Permission granted. Sam has the gift for Elliot?"

"He sure has. Elliot's going to love it."

"Your next shuttle rendezvous is in three hours, so take your time."

"Thank you, sir."

Sarah entered the corridor that extended the entire length of the space station's rotating gravity habitat. On her way to the elevator, heading to the cargo bays, she stopped to look out the giant window. She never tired of the view of Mars. Here in the space station, they levitated high above the northern hemisphere, looking straight down at the Olympus Mons volcano, home to the New London and New Beijing colonies.

She called the elevator. A few seconds later, the doors opened, and she got in. A voice came over the speakers. "Warning, you are about to leave an artificial gravity area. Please enable magnets and hold on."

Sarah lifted her arm and tapped on the screen to enable the magnets in her boots. They snapped to the floor with a satisfying thud. She held onto the rail, and the elevator sped up. After a brief ride, she could feel herself becoming weightless, though her feet remained stuck to the ground. The door opened when the elevator stopped.

The magnets in her boots activated with each footstep, keeping her planted to the ground and preventing her from floating away. Outside the artificial gravity confines of the rotating gravity habitat, walking felt more like creeping. Sarah tried to coordinate her feet and keep her body stable. She reached the entrance to the hangar. The security sensor on the door recognised her as she approached it. It opened automatically.

"Sarah, great to see you again," said Captain Sam Ramirez.

"Hey, Sam," said Sarah as she gave him a hug. "How's the unloading going?"

"Not bad. I should finish in a few hours."

"When are you headed back to Earth?"

"A few weeks. I have some holiday time, so I thought I'd spend it down in New London. A shame to come all this way and not stay for a while." Sam reached into a crate, which was secured to the floor with magnets. "That reminds me. Here's that gift for Elliot. I had to call in a few favours to bring it with me."

"He is going to love this," said Sarah as he handed her a bag. She opened it and pulled out a large hardback book. "*The Collected Works of Sherlock Holmes*. He's really into these old stories. He'll be so excited." There were no trees on Mars, so physical books and paper were rare.

Sam grinned. "You're welcome."

Suddenly, his smile dropped. "Hey, who are you?" He started striding past Sarah. She turned to see a man wearing a balaclava over his head. The man pulled out a small black cylinder from the bag. He pressed a button on the side, and a red light flashed. He thrust the cylinder onto the side of the cargo hatch on the shuttle. It started beeping. Then the man turned around and grabbed a crate. He disengaged his magnetic boots and launched off the ground hard, floating fast towards the cargo bay exit.

Sam turned around in confusion. "Bomb!" someone shouted, and the room, full of cargo workers, erupted into panic. The man had disappeared.

"Everyone out!" shouted Sam. "You too, Sarah."

Sarah stood firm. "I'm in charge of this shuttle when it's docked. We get everyone else out first." The workers disengaged their magnetic boots to reach the door faster. The beeping became a long single ring.

Next, came a deafening bang. The bomb had exploded. A fireball rose inside the shuttle. The metal docking clamps around the shuttle's cargo doors creaked and screeched. A cargo loading arm holding a large crate buckled and collapsed. It pinned Sam to the ground by his leg.

Sarah rushed over and tugged at the loading arm. "I can't move it."

"You need to leave. Now," Sam shouted.

"I can't just leave you."

"You have no…"

There was a massive crunch, and the shuttle shook. Sarah and Sam looked at each other. The shuttle shook again as the clamps disintegrated under the pressure. The shuttle separated from its clamps, exposing the cargo bay to the empty vastness of space.

The loading arm pinning Sam to the ground moved with

the sudden change in pressure. It blew Sam out of the hole and into space. Sarah clung to a handrail with all her strength. Escaping air rushed past her like a hurricane.

With one hand, Sarah managed to open a first-aid box attached to the side of the loading arm, yank out a respirator and shove it in her mouth for some emergency oxygen. The pressure door leading to the corridor outside the loading bay was wide open, exposing the station to the vacuum of space. Sarah reached to the computer on her arm and issued the command to seal the doors.

Relieved, Sarah clutched the handrail, but some debris broke loose and flew towards her, striking her arm. Sarah lost her grip and flew towards the gaping hole made by the destroyed shuttle docking clamps. She clutched at the grating on the floor, her lungs burning as the emergency air supply ran out. Her fingers could no longer hold on, and she was sucked towards the hole and out into space.

## Chapter 1: Football Practice

**Earth Date**: 10th December 2155 - *Nearly two years later*

**_Football Stadium - New London_**

"Okay, team. I want to see your best effort today. Ready for team selection," said Coach as we finished changing in the locker room. Coach jogged on the spot. He was wearing his Martian Rovers football shirt and shorts, with socks pulled to his knees. The Martian Rovers team is just one of many teams in the colony. We love our football here on Mars. I don't think I've ever seen Coach without a whistle around his neck.

"Yes, Coach!" Our entire school team chanted in unison.

I love the game, but I'm not great at it. Coach says I have two left feet. As I said, football is very popular here, as it is on Earth. Some of you reading this on Earth call it soccer. Not sure why, since you use your foot to kick the ball. I'd love to go Earth one day to see a real game played by my favourite team, Manchester United. I've only ever seen recordings. But nobody

## Chapter 1: Football Practice

from Mars goes to Earth because the gravity would kill us. Gravity on Mars is about a third of Earth. Anyone born on Earth would weigh a lot less here. But for us to go to Earth, we would weigh a lot more and our bones would be too weak from our lack of Martian gravity. For now, all I could think about was the day's important match with a school team from the New Beijing colony.

I finished tying the laces on my boots and lined up with the rest of the team.

"One thing," said Coach. "The Chinese team will not have access to their personal A.I. assistants when they join us, so we've agreed that our players will disable theirs, and that starts now. So, no real-time tactical advice." Everyone groaned. Turning off your personal A.I. was like cutting off your arm.

"Watson," I instructed, using my voice to activate the chip implanted into the bone behind my left ear. "Go silent for two hours." I call my assistant Watson because I love old Sherlock Holmes stories from Earth, even though they were written more than three hundred years ago.

"Standby mode activated," replied Watson. Only I could hear him.

"Show me what you've got," said Coach as he led us out through the tunnel. The pitch sprawled out in front of us. The grass was a vivid green, and its sweet aroma blocked the stale smell of the recycled air from the life-support system. Twenty thousand people surrounded the pitch in the stadium, which was covered by a vast glass dome that looked out on the Martian landscape. To one side was the gigantic Olympus Mons volcano.

The atmosphere in the stadium is electrifying when all the seats are full on match days. All the teams in New London play in a league each year. The Martian Rovers won last year. That's

## Chapter 1: Football Practice

who I support. The stadium is one of my favourite places in the colony. It has the second-largest dome in New London. The largest dome is the main atrium and, from it, you can see for miles when a dust storm isn't raging.

My team ran onto the field, and I took up my position in midfield. Coach blew his whistle, and Mikey kicked the ball. Our footballs are heavier than the balls on Earth because of the gravity, so the ball hurtled down the pitch with substantial force. If we used the same balls as Earth, they would just flop around the pitch as they would weigh hardly anything. My team's strikers got straight to work and drove the ball up the pitch, dribbling around the opposing team's defence. Their defence was effective. They took possession of the ball and kicked it back down the pitch. My teammate, Jonny, got the ball and turned to face me. He kicked it, sending it hurtling towards my head. I raised my hands to protect myself. Next thing I knew, the ball was between my hands.

Coach blew his whistle hard. "Are you kidding me, Elliot? This is football. *Foot* ball. The clue is in the name."

"Sorry, Coach," I mumbled.

"It's not the first time, Elliot. You keep on doing it. If the ball goes high, jump and use your chest to drop it to the ground."

"Sorry, it was instinct."

"Instinct. Hmm. If you say so." Coach looked at Dimitri, who was in goal. "Dimitri, come out of goal and swap with Elliot." Dimitri always plays in goal because his size makes him good at stopping the ball. And everyone's scared of him. If you get near the goal with the ball, he just growls at you.

"What?! No. Coach, please. I like it in goal," Dimitri protested.

"You're a fast runner, so I want to try you in midfield," replied Coach.

## Chapter 1: Football Practice

"But I don't want to, Coach."

"Do as instructed, Cadet," ordered Coach.

"But Coach…"

"That's enough, Dimitri. Give me five laps around the pitch."

"But … but…" Dimitri's face turned crimson with anger.

"Do you want to make it ten?" threatened Coach.

"No, Coach." Dimitri left the goal to start his laps. He turned around and gave me a glare. I knew what it meant: you're getting a mega wedgie for this. I needed to stay away from him. And I did feel a little guilty. I took my position in goal.

"Everyone else, resume the game. Tom, take the penalty." Coach blew his whistle.

Tom placed the ball down on the pitch and took a few paces backwards. I positioned myself in the middle of the goal and crouched, ready to pounce at the ball. I locked my gaze with Tom, determined to prove to prove to Coach that I had what it takes. I wanted to be on the team when we played the Chinese. It would be historic.

Tom took his run up and booted the ball. It went left. So did I. I leaped into the air and grabbed the ball, bringing it into my chest as I landed on the ground.

"Great save, Elliot," said Coach. The other team members whooped. Seemed like I made a better goalkeeper than a midfielder. Dimitri was still running his laps. I caught a glimpse of his scowling face. He didn't look happy. Soon, Dimitri finished and came back to the game.

"Swap your shirt, Dimitri, and join the other team," said Coach.

"With pleasure, Coach," he said through gritted teeth. His eyes were still eating into me. Suddenly the idea of being goalie made me feel queasy. What was Coach thinking? He may as well have just let Dimitri beat me up then and there and gotten it over with. I said nothing, though. I hate running laps.

The game continued and I saved three more goals. I was feeling pretty satisfied with myself. Then, as we approached full time, Dimitri got the ball. He charged up the pitch towards me, pushing over anyone who tried to tackle him. Coach blew his whistle, but Dimitri ignored it. He was the largest player on the pitch. Taller than anyone else in our year at school and built like a Martian boulder. All I could do was stand there and wait for the inevitable. He dribbled the ball past our defence, kicked it towards the goal and slammed it hard. It hurtled straight into my face. I dropped to my knees and fell forward. The stadium went dark.

---

I woke up lying on the pitch. The team was staring down at me. Coach knelt beside me.

"You okay, Elliot?" asked Coach.

"I think so. My head hurts."

"I've given you a painkiller shot that will help with the soreness," said Coach as he helped me sit up. "I suggest taking it easy for the rest of the day. If it gets more painful and swells up, go see Doctor Temple."

"I will." I stood up and headed to the changing room to get my uniform back on.

"Okay, team, training is over for today. I'll see you all soon," said Coach.

Once I was dressed in my standard issue dark blue cadets' trousers and blue shirt with the Global Space Alliance logo on the top left, I walked back to the apartment that I share with my dad. Tunnels connect most of the colony buildings. A life-support system that recycles the air we breathe runs through all

## Chapter 1: Football Practice

of them. There's no natural oxygen in the air here. The colony is one giant life-support bubble protecting us from the harsh, toxic Martian atmosphere.

"Watson, disable do-not-disturb mode."

"Do-not-disturb is now disabled," replied Watson, in his computer voice. I keep tweaking his voice. At the moment, he has a British accent, as that is how I imagine Doctor Watson sounding from the Sherlock Holmes stories. "Elliot, I am detecting pain and an elevated heart rate."

"I'm fine. Just a minor accident at football practice."

"Okay, Elliot. I will keep monitoring your vital signs." I continued walking to my apartment. "Elliot, you have an incoming message from Coach. Would you like me to read it to you?" My heart beat a little faster. This was it. Football team results. I closed my eyes tight and crossed my fingers.

"Okay, Watson, read the message."

"Elliot, I have great news. You have made the team for our game against New Beijing. You will be in goal. That was some good goal keeping today. Try not to use your face next time. It's much easier with your hands. See you at the game. Coach," repeated Watson.

"Yes!" I pumped a fist into the air. Other people walking past turned to look at me. "Sorry, I just had some good news." Some smiled, then turned around and went back to what they were doing.

"Well done, Elliot. That was the news you were hoping for," said Watson.

"Thank you. Now, I'm excited."

"I have recognised this. I am monitoring your heart rate and neurochemical levels," replied Watson, like a true computer.

"Always got my back," I said, smiling.

On my way to the accommodation block, I spotted Dimitri

## Chapter 1: Football Practice

with another group of boys. I could feel his icy stare on me. He must have found out about the team results too.

"How's your face, loser?" he called over.

I ignored him and picked up my pace. I was not in the mood for a run-in with the school bully, especially with no teachers around.

# Chapter 2: Chip Reset

**Earth Date**: 11th December 2155

### *Elliot's Apartment*

"Elliot, this is your morning alarm," said Watson. Ugh, it felt too early. I wasn't ready to get out of bed. Five minutes later, Watson tried to wake me again. "Elliot, this is your second morning alarm. Should I schedule in the third and fourth alarms?"

"Okay. I heard you. I'm up. I'm up." I pushed the covers aside and swung my legs off the bed. The daylight panels above my head illuminated, flooding the room with warm, simulated sunlight. A large screen on the wall switched on and displayed some mountains from Earth. Civilian apartments don't have windows, so I like my bedroom screen to show pleasant views when I wake up. I have a different view for every day of the week. Mountains meant it was Tuesday. As my feet touched the floor, the area behind my ear vibrated harshly, followed by a loud buzz.

## Chapter 2: Chip Reset

"Ouch. What's that, Watson?"

"I do not understand the request…" As Watson spoke, his voice buzzed, and I felt pain behind my left ear again. I rubbed the area, and the noise stopped. "Watson, can you book me an appointment at the infirmary?"

"Appointment booked with Doctor Temple for this morning. I have registered a pass from school."

I pulled on my cadet's uniform—an all-in-one suit, with a Global Space Alliance mission badge on the arm and my name and rank (cadet) on the left side of the chest. I walked into the bathroom to brush my teeth. Well, we don't really "brush" here on Mars. Instead, I placed the sonic cleaner in my mouth and bit down to start the ultrasonic cleaning process. When finished, I checked to see if Dad was around, but he had already set off for work at the terraforming plant. He oversees our planetary engineers who are trying to make the Mars atmosphere breathable. His team drill deep down into the Martian surface to access deep pockets of carbon dioxide. Then they pump this into the atmosphere to warm up the planet and make life here a little more hospitable, although Dad said it could take over a hundred years to achieve.

We learned about the climate emergency on Earth in our ancestry lesson. Too much carbon dioxide was leaking into Earth's atmosphere, which caused The Climate Disaster in the twenty-first century. It took a very long time for them to reverse their climate problems. Now we are trying to put carbon dioxide into our own atmosphere to warm up Mars. Everyone who lives here can see the irony. Still, the work my dad and his team are doing is important. I am really proud that we can live here better because of him.

I put my feet in the boots by the door. They cinched tight around my ankles as my heels touched the backs of the boots. I walked up to the apartment door and pressed the button. The

## Chapter 2: Chip Reset

door slid open. I walked out and the door closed and locked behind me.

---

As I approached the infirmary, a man came out of the main doors. He was tall, with short black hair and a standard colony uniform. He barged past me, almost knocking me over.

"Careful," I said as I steadied myself. The man stopped, turned his head towards me and sneered.

"What was that, Cadet Taylor?" he said with a low growl.

I stepped away from him, shocked that he knew my name. He broke eye contact and walked away.

"Watson, who was that?"

"Who was who?" Watson replied.

"The man we just passed."

"There are no people outside the infirmary, apart from you."

"But he was just there. He walked past me."

"I am not showing any tracking beacons in this immediate area except from in the infirmary." As Watson spoke, I felt the buzzing sensation again. I rubbed behind my ear.

"Well, that's strange." I pushed through the infirmary doors and approached the front desk.

"Hello, Elliot. Just take a seat. Doctor Temple will be with you soon," said a voice that filled the room. Our chips track our locations. I was identified as soon as I walked through the door.

"Thanks." I sat down on one of the black plastic chairs in the waiting room and stared at the silent screen on the wall showing the colony news. What is it about screens with the volume turned off that makes you want to stare at them? If you need to see a doctor, and it's not an emergency, then you always wait here. When I was a kid, I once had to wait for

## Chapter 2: Chip Reset

hours to see a doctor. It was so boring; I never enjoy waiting here.

Soon after, Doctor Temple appeared in the waiting room. I enjoy seeing Doctor Temple. She was the same height as me, had green eyes and long blonde hair tied into a ponytail. Her bright personality makes me feel calm every time I come here. Doctor Temple has been my doctor since I was a baby.

"Cadet Taylor. Elliot, how can I help you?" She gestured for me to follow her. "I hope you haven't been trying to stop footballs with your face again?" She smiled at me.

"Oh, you heard about that?"

"I'm afraid so," she said with a grin.

It's quite hard to keep any secrets in this colony.

"How can I help you?" she asked.

"I have been having a problem with my chip. It made a horrible buzzing noise that felt like it was echoing through my body."

"It's possible you dislodged it when you were hit by the ball. Let's have a look." Doctor Temple led me through to a treatment room and pointed to the bed. "Just lie back and relax."

A robotic arm swooped down with a hemispherical attachment that covered my head. As it rotated around my head, I could hear a soft clicking sound. After a few seconds, the robotic arm moved back to its original position.

"Ah yes, I can see here that the chip has detached from the bone a little."

"Oh no, I've never heard of that happening before. Can you fix it?" I asked.

"It happens from time to time. It's not a problem," she said very matter-of-factly. "I'll just disable it and replace it with a new chip. It won't take long."

Doctor Temple reached into a drawer, pulled out a small cartridge and scanned the label with a handheld computer

## Chapter 2: Chip Reset

device. She picked up a small wand-like device and waved it behind my left ear.

"Okay. I have disabled your current chip, so you won't have access to your assistant. I just need to remove the old chip."

"Will it hurt?" I asked. I hate surgery.

"Not at all. I will give you a local anaesthetic, and I can whip it out now." Doctor Temple reached over, picked up an anaesthetic gun and put it over the chip behind my ear. She pressed the trigger and there was a quick hissing sound. The back of my head went numb. "You won't feel a thing now."

I didn't feel the anaesthetic go in, but just knowing it was happening made me hunch my shoulders and wince. Visiting the infirmary is never fun. You just know something is going to hurt by the time you leave.

Doctor Temple picked up another device that looked like a gun. She inserted the new chip into the device and placed it over my faulty chip.

"This won't hurt, Elliot." Doctors always say that. "This machine will make an incision in your skin, extract the old chip and insert the replacement. The machine will also seal the incision."

"I'm ready," I said as I gritted my teeth and closed my eyes.

"I will count down from five," she said. I nodded.

"Five, four, three…" Doctor Temple pressed the trigger on the device. I could feel a pushing and pulling sensation behind my ear.

"There. Done."

"I thought you were counting down to one."

"Was I? Silly me," said the doctor, with a small chuckle. "How did that feel?"

"It didn't hurt, but it felt weird."

"Told you so. The anaesthetic will wear off in an hour." She picked up her wand device and scanned it over my ear. "I have

## Chapter 2: Chip Reset

activated the chip, and it's showing no errors. Try accessing your assistant."

"Watson. Are you there?" I asked. I was nervous, as I was so used to having Watson with me.

"Yes, Elliot. I am active." I exhaled and smiled. Watson has been with me since I was five years old.

"Thanks, Doctor. I can hear him."

"Excellent. Well, you can leave now. If you have any other problems, book another appointment."

"I will." I pulled myself up from the bed. Then I remembered there was something else I'd wanted to ask her. "Oh, Doctor. I have one question."

"Of course. What is it?"

"On my way in here, I saw someone leave the infirmary… someone acting suspicious, like he didn't want me to see his face," I said.

"Interesting," replied Doctor Temple.

"I asked Watson who it was, but he couldn't detect anyone."

"It must have been your chip acting up. I've seen no one else here this morning," she replied. She raised her hand to gesture for me to leave the room.

"Oh. Yeah, maybe." I walked towards the door. "Thanks, Doctor."

"You're welcome. Take care, Elliot."

I left the infirmary and set off for school. If I was quick, I could make it in time for my ancestry lesson.

## Chapter 3: Unity Day

**Earth Date**: 16th December 2155

### *Main Atrium Dome*

Today was the big day. The new train tunnel from New London to New Beijing was set to open. A huge ceremony had been planned. New Beijing has been a separate colony since forever, but now they have joined up with the Global Space Alliance. Dad has been working with New Beijing scientists for a few years already, but now it's time for us civilians to come together. It's exciting. I have never left the confines of New London before. I wonder what it's like over there in the Chinese colony.

    I started the morning by going to the seating area upstairs in the atrium. Mum used to bring me here in the mornings and we would sit and chat before school. We would look out at the mountain range and she would tell me stories about Earth. She always dreamed of going there. I think that's where my Earth fascination comes from. That's until they posted her to the Mars

## Chapter 3: Unity Day

Orbiter station, where she would stay for several weeks at a time. Then, she died in an accident.

I still like to come here in the mornings and daydream about being on Earth, outside and breathing natural air, just as Mum and I used to.

Life on Mars is hard for a kid. You can't just go outside and play because the Martian atmosphere would kill you. Every day in the colony is the same. It's routine, routine, routine. Wake up, go to school, go home, repeat. The views from the atrium are amazing, but I wish I had been born on Earth. They have forests, beaches. On Earth, you can go outside without suffocating and dying an agonising death as your blood boils. It kinda sucks here.

"Watson, tell me the weather in Florida."

"The temperature in Florida is 17 degrees Celsius, which is 62.6 degrees Fahrenheit. It is dry and warm, blue skies, no clouds." I can't imagine what that must feel like. To walk outside on a sunny day and feel the warmth against my skin.

"What's the weather outside the colony?"

"The weather outside New London is -63 degrees Celsius, which is -81 degrees Fahrenheit," said Watson, with his usual deadpan delivery. "There is a category-three dust storm coming our way from the south. We expect it to hit within five days."

Great... Dust storms can last for weeks, and visibility during these storms is almost zero. Plus, the more we terraform the atmosphere, the worse the dust storms seem to get. When our ancestors first landed on Mars, dust storms were very mild. It's the price we pay for trying to create a new atmosphere and they make a real mess on the windows.

I had better enjoy the view while we still have it. Would much rather be in Florida, in the sun, maybe walking through the seawater at the beach. In the old TV shows, the beaches look amazing.

## Chapter 3: Unity Day

Watson's voice broke through my thoughts. "Elliot, you have fifteen minutes until class begins."

Oh no. I had to get a move on. Couldn't be late. I leapt up and ran down the giant spiral staircase to the ground floor of the atrium. I passed the giant statues of the Earth pioneers who helped get us to Mars. They were carved out of rock from the volcano.

"Hey, watch out," said a man carrying coffee from the canteen.

"Sorry," I replied, but I didn't have time to stop.

Reaching the far end of the atrium, I headed down the corridor that led to the education block. I jumped onto the moving walkway but ran anyway to arrive as fast as I could. The corridor to my school is over one kilometre long. As I walked up to the door leading to the classroom, Dimitri was standing there, blocking the door. Just what I needed.

"'Morning, Dimitri," I said. Maybe politeness would defuse the situation.

"So, it's the goalkeeper thief," he said in a low tone. His face wore a twisted grin. Dimitri raised his hands and cracked his knuckles. He wasn't going to make this easy for me.

"About that. It wasn't my idea. Coach moved me into the goal."

"You could have stopped it if you tried."

"How…?" I don't think I'm going to reason with him now.

"Well, how about not saving the goals?" Dimitri stroked his chin like he was explaining a great idea.

"It was team try-outs. What was I supposed to do?"

"How about fail?" said Dimitri. He spat out his words.

"Did you make it onto the team?" I was taking a bit of a risk asking this, but I was interested.

"Yes. I did. Midfield."

"Well, that's good. It'll be an epic game, and you're playing."

"But I wanted to play in goal, and you took it from me."

"It was the coach who took it, not me." This conversation was going nowhere, so I tried to walk past Dimitri.

"Where do you think you're going?" He tried to block me.

"Class. We'll be late."

"I'm always late. I don't care. We'll be late together."

"C'mon, don't be silly…"

"You calling me stupid, Taylor?" Dimitri interrupted.

"No, of course not. I just meant…"

"Nobody calls me stupid." He spat his words out again, and he walked towards me. This was it. I closed my eyes, expecting a punch.

"What's going on here?"

We both looked up. Ms Roberson was approaching us.

"Why are you not in class?"

"I…" I couldn't even get one word out before Dimitri interrupted me.

"Me and Elliot were just talking about our positions on the new football team," said Dimitri, as if we were best friends.

"Ah yes. Congratulations to you both. The game against New Beijing will be so exciting. I suggest you walk into class; otherwise, I will have to mark you both as late."

"Yes, Ms Robertson," we said at the same time. As we walked into the classroom, Dimitri gave me a side-eyed stare and cracked his knuckles again. He didn't need to say anything. This was not over.

---

"Okay, class. I'm afraid that this morning, you'll miss your maths and ancestry lessons," said Ms Robertson. Everyone

## Chapter 3: Unity Day

grinned, glancing around at each other. I'm always happy to dodge a maths lesson. I don't know about ancestry, though. It's one of my favourites. We learn about the history of Earth and our great-great-great-great grandparents who lived there. We also watch a lot of old movies and read old Earth novels. I really like twenty-first-century crime and fantasy stories.

"But don't worry, class. You'll sit your algebra test tomorrow instead. I would hate for you to miss it. I know how much you love maths," continued Ms Robertson with a smile. Everyone sighed.

"Before we head to the opening ceremony, does anyone have questions?"

Becky put up her hand. "Will we be on TV?" she asked.

"Yes, I expect so," Ms Robertson replied. "The news team will broadcast the ceremony all over our colony and New Beijing, and then they'll send it back to Earth. So, make sure your uniforms are neat." Nice. I liked the idea of our pictures being broadcast to Earth.

Dimitri jerked up his hand. "Why is it so important that we join up with another colony? We're doing just fine on our own." He banged a fist on the table. "Why make things more complicated?" Gasps popped around the room. What was Dimitri thinking? Everyone knew we needed unity if we wanted to truly make Mars hospitable. Our ancestry classes had taught us how bad things can get when countries don't work together. Still, I didn't believe Dimitri thought of that, himself. He'd heard it somewhere. It sounded like grown-up talk.

"Because unity is more important than division, Dimitri," replied Ms Robertson, her voice stern. "Everyone, stand up, straighten your uniforms and line up at the door," Ms Robertson ordered. No one grumbled. We all heard her change in tone.

## Chapter 4: The Protest

***Transit Station to New Beijing***

After a short walk from the school and down through the main atrium, we arrived at the new transit station where the shuttles to New Beijing would depart. The new station smelled fresh—a bit like a brand-new rover. Children from all school-age groups stood in rows facing the station. Banners with "*Welcome*" written on them were strung in between metal support beams and children waved Global Space Alliance flags.

On the other side of the station was a large viewing area where other colonists could watch. The area was filling up with people. They all wanted to witness history being made. They spoke excitedly, pointing and scrambling to see, but I couldn't hear what they were saying. As more and more people came into the viewing area, security pushed the temporary barriers back to fit them in.

Lined up in front of the spectators were colony security guards holding transparent full-length shields. The guards stood with the shields extended in front of them, bracing themselves

## Chapter 4: The Protest

to take the force of the crowds should they surge forward. Commander Carter, who is in charge of our colony, was there, as well. The security around the Commander was tight on a normal day; it would be even tighter with the admiral from New Beijing in the same building. Drone cameras hovered in the air, capturing videos for the news team. I made sure to smile in case one faced me.

Next to the shuttle entrance was a large screen. It started a countdown. We all joined in.

"Ten, nine, eight..." everyone chanted. I could feel the gentle vibration of the shuttle pulling closer to the station. "Seven, six, five..." A sign above the closed doors where the shuttle would stop displayed a message: "Shuttle Approaching." "Four, three, two, one." The crowd in the public viewing area pushed forward against the line of security guards. The shuttle stopped outside the door.

It was a long white tube. A loud hissing sound suddenly filled the station. It took me a second to realise it was the pressure normalising in the shuttle. When the doors close, the tube pressurises so passengers can breathe without a surface suit. It makes travel much faster if you don't have to put on a suit each time like we do when we use rovers to travel between buildings. The shuttle doors slid open with a gentle whooshing noise. Then, the protective station doors opened in front of the shuttle. Three men walked out.

"That's Admiral Zhou," said an excited Ms Robertson, as she turned to face the rest of the class. Two security guards stood next to the admiral. They were wearing what looked like formal ceremonial dress uniforms: lots of shiny buttons and medals. Each guard had a holstered energy gun—a weapon that can either stun or kill without compromising the protective shell of the buildings. Admiral Zhou looked even smarter in a formal uniform covered in glistening buttons, tassels and medals. On

## Chapter 4: The Protest

his belt, he wore a sword. Must have been for decoration. There is not much need for swords on Mars. Commander Carter stood in his much-less-fancy commander's uniform, although he had a perfectly waxed moustache that made him look very important. The commander spoke first.

"Admiral Zhou. On behalf of everyone here in New London, I welcome you to our colony on this historic day." Commander Carter held out his hand, and Admiral Zhou shook it.

"We are honoured to visit your colony. We look forward to the close collaboration between our scientists as we work towards our shared goal of terraforming Mars," replied Admiral Zhou.

Both men turned to face one of the drone cameras, smiling and shaking hands. I felt elated. I couldn't stop beaming. This was so cool! Almost everyone was clapping and cheering.

Then I noticed some signs raised in the air. *Say No to Unity. We Are Not Better Together.* The people holding the signs started chanting.

"Say no! Say no! Say no to Zhou!"

Suddenly, more people raised signs, chanting and pushing to the front of the crowd. They surged to the line of security guards—the only thing between the protesters and the commander and his guests.

Ms Robertson turned around. She no longer looked excited. She raised her hand and gestured to some guards who came over and formed a line around our class and all the other classes.

"Where have all these protesters come from?" I overheard Ms Robertson ask one guard.

"I don't know," replied the guard. "They appeared during the countdown and pushed their way to the front." The station

## Chapter 4: The Protest

filled with more and more people. The guards struggled to hold people back. The chanting got louder.

"Say no! Say no! Say no to Zhou!"

"Say no! Say no! Say no to Zhou!"

The protestors stopped merely chanting and started throwing. I couldn't see what they were throwing, but I saw small objects arc their way to the admiral.

The two guards with Admiral Zhou ushered him back into the shuttle, their weapons drawn. The shuttle doors closed, followed by the station doors. I could hear the shuttle pressurising, ready for its journey back to New Beijing. The shuttle pod left the station.

Commander Carter's guards escorted him away, as more security guards appeared. The crowd became even louder.

"Goodbye, Zhou. Off home you go."

"Goodbye, Zhou. Off home you go."

There was rapturous applause from the people at the front of the crowd. The crowds still pushed against the security barriers. Next, the guards with the shields unclipped what looked like black batons from their belts. With a flick of their wrists, the batons extended about a foot in front of them; their ends glowed bright white. Zapper batons! I'd never seen a weapon drawn in the colony before.

Ms Robertson faced our class. "Class, please follow me back to the school."

Then I heard a classmate's cry. "Help," said Alina. She had fallen over in the surge of people trying to leave.

"Are you okay?" I asked, bending to help her up.

"Thanks, Elliot," she replied as she gripped my arm and pulled herself up from the floor. I let her go in front of me as we followed the rest of the class.

I turned for a last look at the protestors. Wait, I knew that face. It was Dimitri's dad. He was holding a protest sign and

## Chapter 4: The Protest

shoving up against the security guards. So that's where Dimitri got his idea from in class ... his dad. Not far behind Dimitri's dad, I thought I recognised someone else—the rude man I saw outside the infirmary. I tried to get a better look, but the crowd streamed around me. I tried to find him again, but he'd disappeared.

---

That evening, I sat in front of the large screen on the wall at home with Dad. The picture extended along the screen to form a hologram.

"Well, that was unexpected today," Dad said.

"I know. Crazy. I didn't see you there."

"No, I was back at one of the terraforming plants. You know, I've been working with Chinese scientists for a few years now."

"How's it going?"

"The collaboration is going well," Dad said. "Their terraforming technology will help make the atmosphere breathable."

"So, why do you think some people are so against us joining colonies?" I asked.

Dad was quiet for a bit. "Fear, mostly, I think. Fear of change. People worry about what they don't understand. Everyone will come around." I nodded in agreement. Dad continued. "Early in the Mars missions, people on Earth protested about going to Mars, saying the scientists should focus on healing Earth and not on going to other planets. Now I bet most people can't even imagine what it would be like to only have Earth. People just need time."

Dad turned up the volume on the screen so we could watch the news report.

## Chapter 4: The Protest

"After today's events at the New London transit station dispersed, Commander Carter took a transit shuttle to New Beijing and continued the planned ceremony," said the reporter. Scenes of Commander Carter shaking hands with Admiral Zhou flashed across the screen. The reporter continued. "While there were small pockets of protest in New Beijing, the opening ceremony has been hailed as an enormous success as our colonies unite."

"Small pockets of protesters," repeated Dad. "From what I heard, it sounded like more than small pockets."

"It was quite scary here in New London. Security even got their zapper batons out," I said.

"I bet it was," said Dad.

I carried on watching the broadcast. "Wow, look how colourful and bright their colony is."

"Brilliant, isn't it? Their colony looks much different to ours."

"I'd love to go."

"We will soon," he replied.

www.ingramcontent.com/pod-product-compliance
Lightning Source LLC
Chambersburg PA
CBHW041136110526
44590CB00027B/4039